the Wealthy way

Don't Go Broke Trying to Get Rich

BY RYAN PINEDA

Published in the United States of America

ISBN: 979-8-9870368-0-8

Published by Ryan Pineda

www.wealthyway.com

*This book is dedicated to all the entrepreneurs
who were told you have to grind and
sacrifice everything to be successful.
There is a better way.*

Scan this QR code to get free
courses, trainings, and tools
to start living the Wealthy Way.

Table of Contents

Listen to this book while you read for free!

Did you know that statistically you are able to retain more information when you both read and listen to a book at the same time?

Well I want to make sure you are able to do just that so I'm going to give you the audiobook *for free*. Go to the link below to instantly get it and listen along.

WEALTHYWAY.COM/AUDIO

Introduction

Mindy moaned as she doubled over, one arm clutching her abdomen as the other supported her weight on the kitchen counter. We'd just finished cleaning the dishes, and I was spent after a long week at work, more than ready to accept the reward of tangling up with my wife on the couch for a bit.

"You all right?" I asked, laying a hand on her shoulder. A dumb question in retrospect—Mindy was not one for drama.

"Ugh, I don't know, my stomach just totally seized up," she muttered. Gradually, she lifted her body upright and leaned into me, gathering herself with a couple of deep breaths.

"Cool?" I asked.

"Yeah, I think I'm good," she replied, music to my ears as we could now return to our regularly scheduled program. But as she trailed behind me toward the couch, it happened again. Except this time, I didn't have to ask. She wasn't all right, and my eagerness to tune out instantly gave way to concern for my wife.

"Something's wrong," she said, but I already knew. We detoured from the couch and headed straight to the hospital.

As Mindy's pain continued to build, so did my speed as I weaved through traffic like an escaped convict trailed by blue lights. The waves were consistent now, the groans from the passenger seat more urgent. We arrived after fifteen minutes which seemed like hours, and right away, they wheeled her into a room where they could examine her.

It was January 20th, 2019, thirty weeks into Mindy's pregnancy, two months until she would give birth to our first child—or so we thought. Removing his gloves and tossing them into the can beside the door, the doctor told us something neither expected to hear: Mindy was in labor.

Ready or Not

I couldn't process what they were telling me. This was not part of the plan. This was not the way it was supposed to go down. I thought: *we don't have a room ready. We don't have clothes ready. We don't have any-*thing *ready. We are not prepared.* I had never felt more dumbfounded.

Then all at once, confusion gave way to a far more dire realization: *our baby might not make it.* And there was little reassurance from the doctors. They couldn't tell me with confidence that the child and the future I had taken for granted leading up to that moment would become a reality.

Thank God, James pulled through and was born a few hours following our arrival, but not without a laundry list of complications. He couldn't breathe or eat on his own. He couldn't do much of anything. One moment, it was life as usual, aside from the excitement and anticipation of soon becoming a new dad, and the next, I was at the hospital where I would spend much of the next few months, looking through the glass of the NICU at my helpless newborn baby.

That turmoil would mark the beginning of the toughest year of our lives and our marriage. And as it would turn out, it was also the birth of my son that would usher in the birth of the Wealthy Way.

My son's premature birth led to a host of developmental delays that demanded around-the-clock attention and care from Mindy and me once he finally made it home. Besides that, although my business had been steadily growing for the past five years, 2019 was panning out to be a difficult year in my professional life.

Yet as push came to shove, I knew in my heart that business had to take a backseat to my family during this season. Instead of doubling down in my efforts at work, I cut back to four-day weeks to be there for Mindy and my son. I started taking Wednesdays off, declaring them "Work-From-Home Wednesdays," the day that I would give my full attention and priority to relieving Mindy of the full-time job of caring for our son. I also took on all middle-of-the-night feedings during that first year, so needless to say, I know what it means to be sleep-deprived.

By the end of James's first year, we had finally found some semblance of normalcy in our lives and our marriage. Sure, our new "normal" consisted of not only the typical perils of infant-rearing—5:00 a.m. wake-up calls, a steady stream of runny noses and dirty diapers, puréed carrots perpetually stuck in my wife's hair, but also a few lingering issues from James's premature arrival. He was progressing, albeit at a delayed pace, but the worst, it seemed, was over.

Until it wasn't.

Derailed

With Christmas just around the corner, the tree lights provided the afterglow to another day of work and parenthood. By this time, James had begun to discover his mobility. No longer confined to a booster seat or a parent's arms, he was ready to get out there and explore.

But as any parent can tell you, a child doesn't make the journey from rolling over to crawling to walking without collecting a few bumps and bruises along the way. Unfortunately, the fall James took on this night nearly derailed the miraculous progress he had made leading up to that moment.

Mindy immediately snatched James up, clutched him tight to comfort him, and scanned his head for injury. At first, it didn't seem so bad—just another bump and bruise along the road to mobility.

But after a few minutes, cautious optimism gave way to alarm when a tennis ball-sized bump formed on his head. James needed to see a doctor, stat.

We were reassured when the doctor told us that all was well. Aside from some tenderness at the spot of impact, he assured us James would be fine. After two days had passed, though, our intuition told us something was not right. The swelling had not gone down, and James wasn't himself. He was lethargic and irritable, not as responsive as we were used to. We could see that we needed to seek a second opinion from another doctor.

The opinion we received threw us right back into the upheaval that had defined the first month of the year. An MRI and X-rays revealed a serious brain bleed that had persisted through the week and required immediate emergency surgery.

To make matters worse, we found ourselves subject to the suspicions and interrogations of Child Protective Services. Though we would later discover this to be standard procedure for the worst-case scenario of child abuse, nothing could have felt more disconcerting at the time. With our son teetering on the brink of life, desperately worried and entirely at the mercy of the doctors tending to James, we were left convincing investigators that we weren't the ones who caused his injuries. All that was left for us to do was to lean on our faith and pray.

Mercifully, all doubts of our love and devotion as parents were cleared, and James survived again. We spent his first Christmas Eve in the hospital and the next day got the best Christmas gift we would ever receive when we brought him home on Christmas Day.

One year of life and one year of losing the luxury of taking the things that matter most for granted. One year that changed my perspective irreversibly. I could see clearly that no matter how much success I achieved in business, no matter how much money I brought in, it was all worthless without the gifts that give life its richness—faith, friends, family, and the health and happiness that we so often take for granted. Life, I learned, should be lived in the spirit of gratitude and with full responsibility for the nurturance of these gifts.

In some ways, all of the hardship we experienced that year turned out to be a blessing. When COVID-19 hit and turned everyone's world upside down, I was prepared for anything. I faced the upheaval head-on, knowing I could cope with whatever came my way after the storm we had weathered in my son's first year. I knew what mattered. I knew what deserved my attention and devotion. With my son on the mend, my values in sharp focus, and my determination and resilience as high as ever, I was ready to bring the Wealthy Way to my life and the world.

The Path to True Wealth

I have been around many people with all the money and status one could dream of, the "ballers" who charter a private plane to their preferred overseas boutique they have reserved so that they could shop for their new diamond-studded Rolex in peace. Yet these same individuals live a day-to-day existence that reflects anything but true wealth.

Behind the scenes, their lives are an utter trainwreck: their marriages are a disaster, their health is in shambles, and they have no faith or purpose guiding their investment of time, energy, and money, nothing to justify the "hustle" that defines their identity. They have pursued financial abundance at the expense of all but their ego, and the result? They are broken, and they are *broke*.

Too often, pseudo-values like hustle, productivity, and profit are placed on the highest pedestal in the business world. But for the person whose values run deeper, these are, at best, means to greater ends, tools in service of the true sources of meaning. Those with a greater purpose hustle when that's what is necessary to support their family.

They produce because they see a need that they have the resources and ability to meet. They seek the profits that will expand their capacity to serve. It's all too easy to lose sight of the deeper "why" when you're immersed in the cultures of business, entrepreneurship, or the one where I got my start, real estate investing. If you're not intentionally prioritizing your values, it's easy to make your business your god.

Though my professional life has evolved dramatically over the last decade, my values and my faith have remained the constants, the foundations on which all else is built. I flipped my first home in 2015. Now, seven years later, I flip hundreds of houses and buy hundred-plus unit apartment buildings. I run seven businesses with the help of the team of superstars that I employ. I produce social media content every day for over a million followers. Despite all of this, I spend more time with my family than ever before, more than when I was struggling to keep my head above water. I'm more involved with my church than I've ever been. I am healthy. I am happy. What I have is *true* wealth, the kind that does not fluctuate at the mercy of my bank account balance or stock portfolio.

This book, and the course that came before it, is, in part, the product of numerous questions and feedback I received from my followers who wondered how I could manage all of these enterprises while also maintaining a healthy family life and a strong faith. They wanted to know how I did it, and I wanted to offer people another way, a life of wealth that extends beyond the mindless pursuit of money.

I wanted to show people that the idea of budgeting, for example, should not apply only to money. Instead, true prosperity is the product of budgeting your time to invest in each aspect of the lifestyle you wish to lead and the person you want to become. This was my inspiration for the WEALTH acronym, each letter representing one aspect of the truly abundant life: worship, education, affluence, lifestyle, team, and health. In part three of this book, we'll discuss each foundational element of true wealth in depth.

For now, what's important to realize and so often forgotten is that there is more to life than money. Of course, this acronym includes an A for financial affluence, but I've seen far too many people spend years chasing money only to discover that it is an empty destination because they neglected the other areas that contribute to a meaningful life. In this book, I will detail step-by-step and principle-by-principle my approach to life, business, and money. I will outline my routine and the role of the WEALTH acronym at its foundation, along with all the ways I budget and invest my time to create a fulfilling life.

I created the Wealthy Way because I deeply desired to share the joy and growth it has brought to my life. The Wealthy Way is a community; it is a philosophy, a toolkit, and a blueprint. It is the culmination of the highs and lows of my journey that ultimately led to the success I have found today, and I truly believe that the principles you will find here hold the potential to change your life and change the world.

PART I

Mindset

CHAPTER 1

Risk and Reward Go Hand in Hand

"Never allow the fear of striking out keep you from playing the game."

—BABE RUTH

In 2010, I was living my dream of playing professional baseball. A lifetime of tenacity from Little League to high school to Division I college finally paid off when, at twenty-one years old, I was drafted by the Oakland Athletics. And that payoff came to the tune of $1,200 a month, five months a year.

Needless to say, I needed more money and something flexible enough to make room for pursuing my true passion, baseball. So that year, I settled on something safe and familiar that I had watched my mom do successfully throughout my life: I got licensed as a real estate agent. I could do this in the offseason, maintain my freedom, and schedule my work around training so that when the time came, I would be baseball-ready. I thought this was the perfect fit.

Unfortunately, the fulfillment and success I enjoyed as a baseball player would not carry over to my career as a real estate agent.

I entered the field on the heels of the financial crisis of 2008 that resulted in low housing prices and gun-shy buyers, far from an ideal recipe for earning commissions. Not only that, but I hated it. I spent days on end showing houses to potential buyers, only to watch them balk at an eighty-five thousand dollar price tag on a home that would have sold in the hundreds of thousands a few years earlier. Again and again, all of the time and energy I invested amounted to zero return.

Truth be told, I had little interest in real estate. My goal was much more ambitious, much closer to my heart, and real estate was only a means to that end. I was a baseball player. And my master plan was simple: get to the big leagues, make millions, and retire.

But baseball was not going as planned, either, and at twenty-three, after three seasons with the Oakland A's, I got a call that would cast doubt on the dream I had been pursuing most of my life. I was being released by the A's.

Uncharted Territory

Until this point, I had followed a familiar set of routines, all built upon a single-minded determination to perform at my best as an athlete. Eight hours of sleep each night, a strict diet, rigorous and consistent training, batting practice, infield drills—everything was centered around making it to the major leagues. And up until my release, that familiarity and that routine worked for me. But now, I was in no man's land, further removed from reaching my ultimate goal of playing Major League Baseball and at a dead end as a real estate agent.

Six months later, I was newly married; my wife, Mindy, was a full-time student with no income, and all I had to show for a lifetime of blood, sweat, and tears and three years as a minor leaguer and real estate agent was a few thousand bucks. After receiving that call from the A's front office, I was complacent with making ends meet through something less-than-ideal, something I could put in my rearview mirror once I made it in baseball. But now, the identity that I'd built my dreams upon and the familiarity of the path that led me to the doorstep of fulfillment was in jeopardy. I could continue to play independent baseball, and it turned out I did just that for another five years, but I knew I needed a backup plan, and I knew for sure that being a Realtor was not it. So I was left with one question: How will I make money? The answer, as it turned out, was right under my nose.

We had recently settled into an apartment, our first home together, but all of this professional upheaval had me feeling anything but settled about how we would pay the rent. With our financial vulnerability in mind, I scoured Craigslist for deals and negotiated my way to furnishing our entire place for about a thousand bucks. I looked around at my haul, feeling quite pleased with what I had gotten at this price: bed frames, mattresses, side tables, a couch, a coffee table, lamps, and some rugs. We had it all, and it looked dang good!

And that's when it hit me, a flash of insight that felt like God grabbing me by the head and holding it in place to understand the potential sitting right before my eyes: I could sell this stuff for three times what I paid for it. Why not do this for a living?

Despite how logical this seemed, it was uncharted territory. The playbook I had relied on to reach the highest level of athletic performance was useless. As far as I knew, no playbook even existed. And in light of our limited savings and income, not to mention my lack of experience doing anything like this full-time, taking action would come with risk. The only way I could test my gut theory was through action. So I put my apprehension aside and leaned into my faith. I sat down at the computer and logged back onto Craigslist. A short time later, I was behind the wheel of a rented truck, a hundred dollars cash in my pocket and a ball of apprehension in my belly, en route to buying the first couch I would attempt to flip.

The Will to Act

Research proves that your body and mind ultimately follow the marching orders of your will. A study out of Finland compared the structure and activation patterns of the brains of low and high-risk-takers.[1] The researchers figured that the low-risk-takers hesitated in making choices so that they could contemplate the wisest course of action. Based on that assumption, they expected to find this group to have more complex neural networks; in other words, they thought that they would be smarter. They ended up finding the opposite.

As a group, the risk-takers displayed significantly more white matter than those who tended to play it safe. Simply put, white matter is the highway system of the brain, the roadways that allow information to travel freely and flexibly from region to region. More white matter, then, means more complex thought. And that means more workarounds, like an elaborate highway system where you can choose between alternative routes to reach your desired destination. The risk-takers had neural networks like a road map of my hometown of Las Vegas; the risk-avoiders, well, their brains looked more like the sleepy desert towns a short drive from the neon lights of the city.

But why would this be? Wouldn't we expect that the sensible ones who consider every potential consequence before acting would be the smart ones? Not if their cautiousness results in paralysis. By definition, we do not know what we will find when we venture into unknown territory, and risks always accompany challenges. But like the body that never labors because it never leaves the couch, the brain that never encounters the challenges that follow risks remains underdeveloped.

---

1 Vorobyev, Victor, Myoung Soo Kwon, Dagfinn Moe, Riitta Parkkola, and Heikki Hämäläinen. "Risk-taking behavior in a computerized driving task: brain activation correlates of decision-making, outcome, and peer influence in male adolescents." *PLoS one* 10, no. 6 (2015): e0129516.

The brains of risk-takers are more developed because they seek out the challenges. They do not sit around contemplating all the consequences and possibilities. They go and find out what they are for themselves. Encounter an obstacle? A traffic jam? The risk-takers find another way around, and if there is not one, they drive through the grass until a new path is worn. They trust that they can adapt, and rightly so. The will gives the marching orders, and the mind and body follow.

Wealth Builders, those who live by the Wealthy Way, take action where others remain stuck in indecision that never leads to action, consumption that never translates to production, and planning that never amounts to execution. The point that seems so obvious but is missed by so many is that you don't get anywhere by standing still in the here and now, forever contemplating what you'll do when there and then get here.

The advantage of "here" for those who avoid risks is that it *seems* safe. What you know is what you can see, smell, taste, touch, and more or less predict based on your habits, the same ways you respond to the same things you see day after day.

But the reality is that just because you choose to stay put does not mean everything else will; "here" will always lead to some unknown regardless of whether you choose to participate. But where you end up does not have to be left entirely to chance. You are not helpless in your ability to influence the outcome. Ultimately, it is you who decides whether the place that you end up happens *to* you, like weeds cropping up as you sit idly in indecision and inaction, or *through* you, the fruits that spring from your decisions and actions. True, nothing is guaranteed, but you improve the likelihood of getting what you want from the future if you take steps in that direction. Inevitably, you choose your risk.

Risking Exposure

The risk avoider's unwillingness to confront their fear of the unknown leaves them unwittingly handicapped. Even though they might feel unhappy with their current circumstances, bored, lonely, and jaded by life in a one-stoplight town, they reason that at least it is safe here. Their discontent is outweighed by the fear that they will get swallowed up if they venture outside of what they know, so they do nothing. And doing nothing might work to ensure safety in the short term. Sure, it would be scary to try something new. But guess what? Fear feeds on avoidance.

But the opposite is also true. The cure for fear of taking risks is the same as for any other fear: exposure. When a person seeks out the assistance of a therapist to overcome a phobia—spiders, let's say—then they will be gradually and repeatedly exposed to some representation of spiders until they realize whatever horrible consequence they imagined would occur if they encounter a spider never actually happens.

So, for example, a therapist might start by encouraging the arachnophobe to simply imagine and discuss what it would be like to encounter a spider, an exercise that at first might arouse a good deal of fear but after a while becomes quite unarousing, even boring. Next, the therapist might have him watch a video of a spider. After that, he will observe a live spider from another room and then in the same room. Eventually, the person who initially believed he was incapable of bearing so much as the thought of spiders may find that he can allow one to crawl on his arm without consequence or fear. In other words, what initially seemed incredibly risky turned out to be quite mundane.

Ultimately, each step of exposure requires an act of faith that you can handle whatever obstacles and challenges may arise as you step into the unknown. And faith, whether in God or yourself, serves as a means and an end. Faith fuels the will to act, and acting on your will further fuels the faith that inspires the actions to come: bolder ones with greater risks and greater rewards. As it turns out, faith precedes and proceeds the will to act.

Action Items

At the foundation of all fears lies risk: risk of failure, risk of humiliation, risk of losing control, all the way down to the risk of death. When coupled with avoidance, that fear exaggerates every risk and imagined consequence until no reward beyond the safety of the status quo seems reasonable. But the truth is that risk also accompanies every great triumph—not triumph over fear but triumph *despite* fear. Below are some ways that you can embrace risks in the face of fear and discover the rewards that lie beyond the status quo:

1. **Find a side hustle.** Couch flipping, house flipping, car sharing, grocery shopping for others—the options are endless. What starts as extra income may well become enough to make a living. This is the area of life where you can try new things and experiment. Start small and scale.

2. **Embrace exposure.** Like the arachnophobe who can't bear the thought of a spider, start small. Confront the thought you can't bear, then take a small action. Whatever it is you might be avoiding, whatever big scary goal has you stuck in inaction, choose one small step, then another. Next thing you know, you might find yourself petting that big, scary spider.

3. **Focus on the experience, not the end result.** It's easy to fall prey to the tendency to view failure as evidence of inability, but the road to ability is paved with failure. Mastery results from a long series of unmastered attempts followed by reflection on how to get a little better the next time. Practice, but do so with intention. Consider where you fall short and apply these reflections on how you approach whatever skill you're trying to improve and

whatever goal you're striving to achieve. The end result will take care of itself, even if it isn't what you intended. Despite falling short of achieving my dream of making the big leagues, the life lessons and personal growth I gained along the way were invaluable. Embrace the journey.

The Will to Risk

I arrived back home with the couch in tow and, much to the dismay of my wife, crammed it into the already-limited space of our tiny apartment. It was time to test my theory. I gave the couch a little spot-cleaning, snapped a few photos, and posted it right back on Craigslist for three hundred dollars more than what I paid for it. A few days later, the couch sold at the asking price, no questions asked. That was my aha moment. The risk of stepping out on faith to try something completely new had paid off, and that was all the proof I needed to go bigger and bolder.

Within weeks, I had taken what little we had saved up and bought an old beat-up GMC Sierra (that I later discovered had an altered odometer that displayed far fewer miles than she had actually traveled) for fifteen hundred dollars, rented a 10x30 storage unit to hold my inventory, and was off and running on my first foray into entrepreneurship.

Right out of the gate, couch flipping was a success. I bought and resold everything I could find that was undervalued and brought in a thousand dollars a month. I realized pretty quickly that my earnings were limited only by my ability to store everything I bought. So I went bigger. I expanded to multiple storage units to keep up with demand. I figured out what type of couch brought it the most profits (it's sectionals, by the way). Feeling like a big-timer, I even upgraded to the 2004 Toyota Tundra that I would replace and give to my dad a few years later. One thousand dollars became two thousand, two thousand became four until eventually, I made eight thousand dollars net profit every single month. What began as an experiment had turned into a full-fledged living.

Despite bringing in more money than I ever had and doing it on my own terms, my success came at a price. I started to get burned out. When I was just starting out, my hopes of making the major leagues had been dashed by my release from the A's, and I had reached the end of an unfulfilling and unsuccessful stint as a real estate agent. With the stakes high and my confidence low, buying a single couch to resell presented a risk, not just to our meager savings but also to my bruised ego. So turning a profit on it felt like a life raft, delivering an exhilarating release. I could breathe. This offered a temporary relief on the back end of disappointment, a renewed sense of direction, and quick, reliable profits; it offered "success."

A year later, I had a full-scale business with a delivery truck, multiple storage bins, and enough couches to fill each one wall to wall. And despite that, buying couches had become... boring, like watching a spider crawl around in the next room.

Besides that, couch flipping was a grind, one that initially grew out of urgency and necessity and one intended as a side hustle, not an endgame. I held no delusions of flipping couches as a career. Sure, I had begun to find what felt like financial prosperity given the scarcity I had grown accustomed to, but internally, I knew something was awry.

Put simply, I was not proud of what I was doing, and I knew in my heart that I was meant for something more. It was time for a change of direction, but I was no clearer about where to turn than I had been a year before when I had embarked on this crazy couch-flipping journey.

This internal restlessness culminated when Mindy and I visited New Orleans for our first anniversary. A year removed from my unceremonious release from the A's, I got a long-overdue breather from the endless hustle of flipping couches. As I reflected on my place in life, I silenced my anxiety and turned to the Lord to show me my next move. Kneeling on the gray carpet of our hotel room, hands folded on the bed, I asked, "Jesus, what do you want me to do with my life?" Little did I know that I would someday look back on that prayer as the turning point of my life.

CHAPTER 2

Leap Enough and You Learn to Fly

"Action separates the heroes from the cowards, the achievers from the complainers, the successful from the mere dreamers, the happy from the envious; it separates those who rise to the challenge of their goals from the haters who cower in the shadow of stagnancy."

—STEVE MARABOLI

C ouch flipping gave me a taste of the entrepreneurial life. It started when I dipped my toe in and bought a single couch to attempt to flip, an experiment that proved it to be as simple as I had imagined. The next thing I knew, I was waking each day like the Michael Phelps of the couch-flipping world, leaping in headlong, dragging couches behind me, then doing that flip-turn thing, cash in hand at the end of each sale, ready to retrieve another. I had scaled what started as a simple experiment into my first successful business. I had systems in place. I was good at what I was doing, and I was making good money doing it. I was driven. I was self-reliant. I was stable.

But swimming like that from sunup to sundown is not sustainable. I was exhausted, waking each day to the endless grind of maintaining the systems and routines I had put into place to keep us afloat. I was jaded, using my talents to chase profits at the expense of purpose, relying on the force of will to push past hesitancy of spirit. And I was discontent, having watched my self-reliance carry me only to the point where stability meets stagnancy. Yeah, I had jumped in and started swimming, but there was no end in sight to this race.

All the while, I was preoccupied with a fantasy that for years had visited my conscience without invitation: if only I had money, I could make a killing flipping houses.

Put Me In, Coach

The most maddening thing about my time as a Realtor was finding all of these once-in-a-lifetime deals that go along with a recession, only to watch the potential buyers walk away. The magnitude of opportunity lost on the risk aversion of these people truly baffled me, and it was painfully clear the money I could make if I was in their position.

But even after a year of flipping couches, I still was not there. I did not have the money necessary for a down payment on a house, so my house-flipping fantasies always led back to my present reality, chasing money to pay our bills. Stuck at that familiar dead-end on that day in New Orleans, I turned to Jesus for guidance.

Well, no sooner than I had uttered amen did I turn on the television and come across a commercial with a man claiming that he had the secret to flipping houses with *no money*. Of course, I felt immediate skepticism—this had to be a scam. Fortunately, though, my intrigue exceeded my doubt. If this were true by some wild chance, it would quite literally be a dream come true.

So I did what you do: I consulted Google, and it told me to check out BiggerPockets. Over the next several days of fervent scouring, this website taught me everything real estate class didn't: house-flipping, wholesaling, rentals, and on and on. I learned that there are, in fact, ways of buying houses with no money. And that is all it took. I was off to the races, reading everything I could get my hands on, anything that would show me how to turn yesterday's pipe dream into tomorrow's reality.

A Chance Encounter

By the time Mindy and I were set to board the plane back to Vegas, my excitement to put what I was learning into practice had reached a fever pitch—I was ready to get home and crush it. So when I found out Mindy and I would be sitting separately because we'd skimped on assigned seating, I jumped at the opportunity to pull out my Kindle and dive right back into one of the books I was reading, a how-to on house flipping.

After a few minutes immersed in what I was reading, I was interrupted by the voice of the old man sitting next to me, whose presence I had been practically oblivious to until now.

"Hey, what are you reading?" he asked.

I explained that I planned to dedicate myself to house-flipping upon my return from our anniversary and that this was one of the books I was reading to guide my efforts.

The conversation that followed is one I'll never forget. This stranger, the one assigned to the seat I had anticipated Mindy would occupy, had a message for me.

After a thoughtful pause, he spoke. "Listen, I don't really talk to a lot of people on planes, much less offer prophecies." Another pause. "But I just feel God's calling me to tell you that you're going to be very successful in this, and you're going to change lives doing it."

Of course, this is not what anyone expects from a casual conversation on an airplane, but he certainly had my attention. And he wasn't done.

"I've been in real estate for many years and flipped countless homes, and I can tell you that there are more ways to flip homes now than ever before—even if you don't have a lot of money," he said.

I couldn't believe what I was hearing! Much of what came after that was a blur, but every bit of insight he offered only solidified my decision further and strengthened my conviction and confidence about the season to come.

Before we parted ways, he gave me his phone number and email, encouraging me to reach out if I ever needed anything. A short time after that, I took him up on that offer, and he sent me some resources that were frankly over my head at the time. But he had already offered me an absolutely priceless gift. He had stoked the fire on the path I was about to embark on and turned it into a blazing inferno.

Chasing the Dream

I never anticipated in the year leading up to my anniversary that the hours on end of scrolling through Craigslist, negotiating with sellers and buyers, and loading and unloading couches had prepared me for this discovery. As it turned out, all the hustle sharpened my discernment about what constitutes a good deal and how to recognize overlooked value and potential for restoration. I was learning how to run and scale a business. Most importantly, my boldness and willingness to take risks were growing alongside my business and profits.

So when Mindy and I returned to Las Vegas, I was uniquely positioned to seize the opportunities I'd discovered. One of the things I learned about in my crash-course self-education was the idea of a hard money loan. If you're not familiar with this type of funding, a hard money loan is a high-interest loan that comes from non-traditional lenders or from individuals—where your value is determined not by your credit score or your income but by the quality of the deal that you can find. So just as I had done with couch flipping, I could make money if I found a good deal.

By this time, I had already found the deal, one I thought was a home run. I also had ten thousand dollars saved from couch flipping that I was ready to pay down. I just needed to find my investor. So I called every hard-money lender in Las Vegas until I eventually found *one*. Only as it turned out, I didn't have enough money. I was a new flipper, a higher liability, and I would need 20 percent down to secure the lender's contribution. In other words, I was thirty thousand dollars short.

And then, in 2014, short on funds but teeming with conviction and determination, I went all in. I knew the price of admission, so I ignored the urging of friends, family, and fears to stay the course of safety and stagnancy and did what was necessary to get into the game. I applied for every credit card under the sun, not just in my name but also in Mindy's. The result was fifty thousand dollars in credit: enough to transfer the balances toward my first flip and have some leftover if it didn't work out. Then, it was time to make the deal. That day, I flung the raft aside and started swimming.

The Cost of Stability

An elite professional baseball player will get a hit about three times out of ten at bats. He might hit one out of the park once out of twenty at bats. But even that level of success will not happen unless he keeps stepping up to the plate and taking his cuts every time the opportunity presents itself. And guess what happens in the process? The more that person shows up, the better he sees the pitches, the smoother and more powerfully he swings, the more his confidence grows, and the higher the ratio of success to failure becomes.

Of course, the risk of failure, swinging mightily and missing completely, accompanies each endeavor. But what is the alternative to risk? So-called stability? Well, maybe that is enough for you—nothing ventured, nothing lost. But stable has two meanings. One is "constant and reliable." The other is "an enclosure where domestic animals are kept."

Every attempt at something new requires a leap of faith. Depending on where you are on the journey, that leap might look more like a hop. For the person caught in the throes of depression, leaving the house might require total exertion of their will. For me, buying a one-hundred-dollar couch felt like a big deal at one point.

When I saw the opportunity to turn my wishful thinking into practical action, I considered the risk of staying the course higher than venturing into the unknown. All in on cash and maxed out on credit, I considered the worst-case scenarios: maybe I would declare bankruptcy or lose it all and have to pay it back. Needless to say, those outcomes would have sucked, but guess what? I had the time and energy to double down on my efforts and dig myself out of my hole if it came to that.

But more than anything, taking the leap of faith put me on the path of growth, facing challenges and lessons that otherwise would have remained conjecture. Had I stayed the course, maybe found a steady job, I would have always wondered what lay beyond my life of stability, where I was safe, stable, like an animal confined to its enclosure.

The Futility of "Later"

I could have waited until I was more "settled" to flip my first home. I could have sat on the sidelines until the market crashed, waiting for something I'd heard "experts" predict for years. I could have told myself I would take the leap later when it was safer. But more than likely, I would have been lying to myself. Beneath all of the ways we rationalize, a delay is an implicit declaration of faithlessness in ourselves that prevents us from going after what deep down we know that we want now, not when it is safe.

And the truth is that the stakes become higher, not lower, as time passes. With every day handed over to delay, you will have less time and energy to invest in recovering from a setback. And maybe you plan to marry and have kids as you get older. Well, they will have to bear the weight of recovery if it does not work out for you.

And as the years go on and the stakes increase, it's a fact that your propensity to take risks decreases alongside it.[2] Playing it safe is a habit that gets harder and harder to break. A study examining the relationship between risk-taking and age determined that older adults are no less motivated than younger people to avoid losses but are far less willing to take the risks that may result in big rewards. This aversion to risk occurred parallel to declines in dopamine, a neurotransmitter responsible for predicting what actions will result in rewards and one that steadily decreases with age. In other words, as you age, your brain becomes less opportunistic and less likely to recognize and execute the bold actions that will produce bold results. So if you are unwilling now, the chances are even higher that you'll be unwilling down the line when you *are* settled in and used to the safe confines of your everyday life. The older you get, the more convinced you will become of the futility of wishing for something more.

---

2   Rutledge, Robb B., Peter Smittenaar, Peter Zeidman, Harriet R. Brown, Rick A. Adams, Ulman Lindenberger, Peter Dayan, and Raymond J. Dolan. "Risk taking for potential reward decreases across the lifespan." *Current Biology* 26, no. 12 (2016): 1634-1639.

Choose Your Regrets

According to author and TED Talk presenter Kathryn Shulz, regret involves the convergence of two elements.[3] Agency is the first, the belief that a person could have chosen differently. The second is imagination, the ability to envision having used that agency to make a better choice that would have led to a better outcome and, therefore, a better present.

The pain of regret can be a powerful teacher. The glaring emotional consequence reveals how much you cared about the opportunities you squandered through your carelessness. The potential value of regret is that it can serve as a source of insight, calling our attention to the mistakes that were made and the cost that they imposed so that we will never be so shortsighted again.

But what about the opportunities that knocked and eventually left to never return because you wouldn't answer? What about the dreams that constantly pleaded for you to just *try* and see what happens? What is there to learn when the opportunity has passed and it's too late to chase the dream?

The answer is not much, which is why regrets of inaction are far more common than those of action. Asked to name their greatest regret, 76 percent of people point to the things they could have done to make them the people they now realize they could have been.[4] And as it turns out, the regrets of what we didn't do not only last the longest but progressively worsen over time. The opportunity is lost, and the dream is dead. Nothing ventured, nothing earned, nothing learned, and no way forward.

---

3   Kathryn Shulz, "Why We Should Embrace Regrets," NPR, May 2, 2012, https://www.npr.org/transcripts/151886493.

4   Shai Davidai and Thomas Gilovich. "The ideal road not taken: The self-discrepancies involved in people's most enduring regrets," *Emotion*, 18, no. 3, (2018) 439–452. https://doi.org/10.1037/emo0000326

When I was flipping couches, I dismissed the idea of making it big in real estate investment as a pipe dream. I had the imagination but not the financial means. But when I discovered the means, I had a choice: continue on the path toward stability, something safe and predictable, or take the key I'd been handed to open the door to the dream that had resided in my heart for years leading up to this moment. I chose the latter. I saw the opening, and I made a run for it.

Action Items

What greater tragedy is there than that of unfulfilled potential, the life story lived only in the mind of its intended hero? If the value of regret is the opportunity to learn from our past mistakes, then the value of dreams is to point us toward the possibilities of our future. We have to take those dreams seriously, more seriously than the doubts and fears that lead to regrets that offer no path to redemption. We must have faith to move in the direction of our dreams. Here are some ways you can start now:

1. **Identify your dreams.** A famous Chinese proverb asserts, "A journey of a thousand miles begins with a single step." Well, that's true, but before that, you need to determine the destination you desire so deeply that you would travel a thousand miles to get there. Too often, we dismiss the future we want most to avoid acknowledging our disappointment with the present. So spend some time thinking about the dreams you have abandoned. Then pick one, and write down every detail of how you're feeling and what you're doing in your dream. Then take the first step past the doubts and fears that lead to regret and into the faith that leads toward the life of your dreams.

2. **Foster a growth mindset.** Your leap of faith is just the beginning; a life beyond stability is not supposed to be safe or easy. Reframe challenges and failures along the way as opportunities

to grow. Trade regrets of inaction with regrets of action, the kind that can be course-corrected by faith in your ultimate destination. Recognize that it is normal to struggle at something new and that perseverance precedes change.

3. **Leverage regret.** We can only leverage the feeling of regret when we uncover the thoughts beneath the surface, thoughts that can pave the path to a better outcome the next time opportunity knocks. In fact, research demonstrates that processing our regrets through writing or even speaking into a voice recorder weakens their emotional hold on our present and leverages their power to reshape our future.[5] In his book *The Power of Regret,* Daniel Pink explains it this way: "When feeling is for thinking, and thinking is for doing, regret can perform its decision-enhancing, performance-boosting, meaning-deepening magic."[6]

Failing Forward in Faith

I failed in my effort to make it to the major leagues. The result was that I carried discipline built through the grind of professional sports into my daily life and business. I failed as a real estate agent. From that failure came confidence in my skills as a deal-maker and an understanding of real estate transactions that would give me a leg up when I found my way into house flipping. In couch flipping, I failed to find a sense of satisfaction and pride in what I was doing. Consequently, I learned to scale a business and continued to sharpen my ability to recognize and negotiate a deal.

---

5   Lyubomirsky, Sonja, Lorie Sousa, and Rene Dickerhoof. "The costs and benefits of writing, talking, and thinking about life's triumphs and defeats." *Journal of personality and social psychology* 90, no. 4 (2006): 692.

6   Daniel Pink, *The Power of Regret* (New York: Riverhead Books, 2022), 170.

And here's the doozie, couched in a bit of a spoiler (pun intended). About a decade after my initial foray into couch flipping, I would go on to find considerable success in social media, amassing over a million followers largely thanks to a few widely-viewed videos on the subject of, you guessed it, couch flipping.

The culmination of all these "failures" was to perfectly equip and position me to respond to God's call when He presented me with the opportunity to enter the big leagues of real estate investment, the dream I'd been carrying for years. In retrospect, I had been training for my opportunity, and I had not gotten the call to duty until it was one that I could answer.

As it turned out, my faith would be further tested when I found another house just two weeks after I bought my first. It was too late to turn back now—I was either going to crash and burn or take flight. But destiny was on my side. After six months flipping houses and forty thousand dollars in profits, I had just made what would have taken me a year of grinding as a baseball player and Realtor, five months of non-stop buying, picking up, refurbishing, and reselling couches. I was stunned.

Little did I know, I was just getting started. I kept my credit card maxed and bought three more that year, reinvesting the profits into the next deal and the next. I would flip five homes my first year, twenty my second year, and fifty the year after that, before skyrocketing to 150 flips in my fourth year.

Needless to say, the success of this first leap of faith set in motion a chain of events still unfolding. One moment, I'm hatching a wild plan to make ends meet by reselling couches, and a few years later, I'm running seven businesses, still flipping houses like crazy, and producing social media content every day for over a million followers.

I did not expect to own all of these businesses. I didn't expect to be creating content, much less broadcasting it to an audience of millions. I didn't even have plans to flip five homes the first year, just as I didn't expect to buy so many couches that I would need multiple storage units.

The common denominator was leaps of faith that catapulted me to entirely different playing fields and showed me opportunities that simply did not exist in the safety of the routine or making "enough" money. Yes, taking on a new game presents new challenges, but on the other side of a leap of faith lie opportunities and rewards you couldn't have fathomed. You will never know unless you try, and you will wonder forever if you do not. For every person whose success you covet, you will find someone who proceeded boldly in the direction of their conviction.

For me, it all started with faith—faith in what I felt God had invited me to do despite no promises of where my willingness might lead. And I am glad the surprises were not spoiled because they exceeded my wildest dreams when I emptied my bank account, maxed out our credit cards, and went all in.

I'm not just talking about faith in God but in yourself. Each new venture requires an investment, an outward expression of your faith in yourself or God. Growth, by definition, takes you places you have never been before. So try something new and bold; make an investment, hire a new person or a coach, and invest in yourself and your growth. Leap into a new playing field with faith that you will learn the rules when you get there.

Decide now if you want to go further. The Wealthy Way is not for those who are content to be ordinary and obedient to the rules set by others but for the extraordinary who create the rules. I get it. You're in your twenties. You feel you are behind. You see others experiencing the success you want to experience—people pulling in hundreds and thousands of dollars, and you cannot seem to find any traction whatsoever. Certainly, that was me.

But with sober self-reflection, openness to considering another way, and a few leaps of faith, I found my profession taking on a life beyond me and the reach of my day-to-day actions. In what seemed like a blink of an eye, I was running seven businesses that produced millions in revenue, churning out social media content for over a million followers, all while maintaining my turnaround in house flipping. In 2014, I flung the raft aside and started swimming. But now? Now I was walking on water.

Book a free strategy call with my team today.

I created the Wealthy Way Academy as a modern way for people to develop the skills needed to build wealth. You don't need to rack up student loan debt, climb the corporate ladder, or look for your next job. You can learn skills and start building wealth immediately without doing any of that.

If you want to be mentored by my team and me on things like real estate investing, social media content creation, and entrepreneurship, you need to join us. We have coaching programs, events, and so much more.

Visit the link below to book a free strategy session with my team. Let us help you figure out what path will be most effective for you to start building wealth.

↓

WEALTHYWAY.COM

CHAPTER 3

Discipline Is a Muscle

*"Discipline is choosing between what you want now
and what you want most."*

—ABRAHAM LINCOLN

Minor League Baseball was like boot camp, a game of attrition to weed out the faint of heart. The endless travel on a cramped bus, the inevitable ups and downs of performance, the estrangement from loved ones, not to mention you're paid peanuts. It all begged the question, how committed *are* you?

That was a far cry from my journey to get there. The line between practice and play was blurred, and "discipline" was a natural product of my passion for the game. It was simple. The school bell signaled the end of my day as a student and the start of my day as a baseball player. Free time meant practicing baseball, watching baseball, talking baseball–living and breathing baseball. Sure I had dreams of playing in the major leagues, hearing the roar of the crowd when I hit the game-winning home run or made the diving catch, but I played and practiced baseball because I loved baseball and wanted to be the best at it.

But I wasn't a kid anymore. I was an adult, and that dream had become a goal that was suddenly within my reach. The season lasted for five months out of the year, so for the remaining seven months, I was on my own to prepare my mind and body for the next season and make enough money to survive. There were no coaches to set a practice schedule and assign drills to sharpen my skills, no teammates to play alongside me and hold me accountable for showing up and trying hard, and no pats on the back for a well-done job. What's more, my mom and dad weren't around to put food in my belly and a roof over my head. All of that depended on me and my will to succeed.

But will without a plan gets you nowhere. Though all those resources were no longer at my disposal—ample free time, the constant presence and support of coaches, teammates, and parents—I learned that growth springs from routines and habits, in fits and starts and at its own pace. Only now, no one would make sure I gave it my all and gave it consistently but me. Now, I was boss and employee, coach and player. So, with all my many responsibilities and the limited time available to uphold them in mind, I set my intentions. I chose my disciplines. And this meant committing the first hours of each day to baseball.

Knowing I had limited time, I woke up super early each morning. I went to the gym and worked out for an hour and a half, doing sprints, lifting weights, and performing all of the exercises that would translate to my performance on the baseball field. Then, I went straight to the batting cages to hit for an hour and then onto the field to take ground balls and throw for an hour. Only after fully investing in my passion did I turn my day toward doing what I had to do to supplement the twelve hundred dollars I got to support my dream—from meeting with potential real estate clients to flipping couches and, eventually, flipping houses. It was that way day after day, religiously doing workouts in the morning and commencing my workday in the afternoon.

All this training and commitment was preparation for the real challenge—the remaining five months of the year, which consisted of 140 games in five months. You can do the math—it's a lot. Those five months were when all my physical and mental strength would be tested, and my degree of discipline leading up to those five months was either rewarded or punished. During this period, anything resembling a daily routine was thrown out the window, yet at the same time, every day felt like Groundhog Day. Nevertheless, the "typical" day went something like this.

I woke at nine or ten in the morning, depending on how late I arrived home from the ballpark. "Home" might be my bed in my bedroom, a generic discount-hotel chain, or the bus to the next city. If I was lucky, I squeezed in a workout before I ate and then headed back to the ballpark. At the ballpark, I went through the pre-game motions of batting practice and fielding ground balls before our 7:00 p.m. game time. We played until 10:00 p.m. I tried to go to sleep around midnight—if I was lucky.

In reality, it was rare that things played out in any way that could be called typical. Maybe this routine was possible for a home game. But when we were on the road, rolling into Wichita, Kansas for a game, all red-eyed and disoriented, with no clue where to eat, let alone work out, good intentions got thrown right into the dingy hotel room trash can. There were bus rides that took more than twenty-four hours. There were minor league teams who refused to invest in buses equipped with sleeper seats, leading my teammates and me to resort to buying pool rafts from the general store to blow up and arrange along the floor to try and get some rest before the next game in the next city. True story.

Those three to four hours of committed action that started each day during the off-season and the time I squeezed in between the chaos of the minor league season represented my commitment to myself and the path I had chosen. They formed the foundation of my self-respect. At the end of the day, I could look at myself in the mirror and lay my head down on a soft pillow (or a Walmart raft) knowing that I had given my all to my chosen path. And, unbeknownst to me at the time, those hours of committed action would set a precedent for the level of discipline that I bring to business today.

The Danger of Diversion

Of course, I was tired. Of course, I got discouraged. Of course, I woke up to sore muscles or a crick in my neck from sleeping on a raft. Each time they arose, all of those very real feelings made a convincing case to neglect the commitments I'd made to myself. But I knew what I wanted to accomplish, where I wanted to get, and who I wanted to become, and I knew that I would only get there through a radical, unconditional commitment to my path.

Let's say you're working a job that you don't like. You come home from work tired, discouraged, maybe even demoralized. When you feel like that, with just a few hours to yourself, all you want to do is check out. As I have mentioned before, I hated being a real estate agent, so that was definitely the case with me outside of baseball.

Checking out offers a substantial reward: immediate and reliable relief. But in the end, what you are reinforcing is a behavior that doesn't take you anywhere. Ultimately, checking out leaves you stuck and leads you right back to the doorstep of where you wanted to escape. Checking out pauses living and responsibility—until bedtime, when you (again) wait for the alarm clock to force you back into the nightmare you were trying to escape through distraction.

"If I can just get through this day, I can unplug and tune out," you might say to yourself. Or, you can find a way out of an unsatisfying situation and into a rewarding one, one you don't want to escape. Instead of giving your focus away to some diversion, you can turn it toward endeavors that mean something to you that will leave you feeling proud of your efforts and bring you closer to where you want to be and who you want to become. Maybe you work toward finding a new calling that aligns with who you are, something that feeds your spirit instead of eating away at it little by little, day after day.

Yes, it was hard to wake up and do everything I had promised myself I would do with no one telling me what to do and no immediate consequences for not showing up. Yes, I felt tempted to stay in bed, give myself a day off, and give a halfhearted effort at the gym or on the practice field. But, ultimately, I knew that I would only be shortchanging myself.

Your Loudmouth Companion

The harsh truth is that you will always have to listen hard for the voice of determination through the noise of resistance. The constant loudmouth companion on your journey toward achieving your goals is the desire to escape to a situation that offers less resistance and less potential for failure.

In one study demonstrating this phenomenon, participants were fitted with beepers that randomly cued them to report whether they were experiencing resistance or desires competing with their goals and intentions at any given moment.[7] Of the ten thousand responses provided by participants, *seven thousand* reported the presence of something calling them away from their intended action.

In other words, resistance doesn't go away. The feelings you use to justify it "not being the right time" to stay on track toward some personal conviction or aspiration cannot be counted on as reliable guides

---

7   Hofmann, Wilhelm, Roy F. Baumeister, Georg Förster, and Kathleen D. Vohs. "Everyday temptations: an experience sampling study of desire, conflict, and self-control." *Journal of personality and social psychology* 102, no. 6 (2012): 1318.

to your actions. If you wait until they are absent, you will spend most of your life waiting to start, and those starts will be followed closely by stops short of growth. You won't be consistent. You won't be disciplined. You will be at the mercy of your whims, gullible to the loudmouth's claims that you are too tired, too discouraged, or too sore to do what you committed to doing.

The Self-Control Muscle

Skill in baseball, just like any other sport, develops through repetition. Muscle memory happens after many opportunities for a group of muscles to remember what they are being asked to do. The result once everything sinks in is automaticity; the task becomes second nature and requires far less strain and thought.

As it turns out, self-control, the engine that drives discipline, works much like muscles. It is by pushing through resistance that a person is eventually able to run faster, throw farther, and hit harder. The exercise of discipline requires you to continually push through resistance, just as you do with physical exercise. And discipline requires you to be your own source of accountability, overriding the desires and feelings that compete with whatever you have decided you want to do. And as I have noted, that competition nearly always exists.

Social psychologist Roy Baumeister proposed an explanation and solution for this phenomenon called the Strength Model of Self-Control.[8] Baumeister defined self-control as the ability of an individual to override primary desires, i.e., the loudmouth, to bring actions in line with good intentions. His research suggests that the brain responds to pursuing your goals in the face of temptation like

---

8   Baumeister, Roy F., Kathleen D. Vohs, and Dianne M. Tice. "The strength model of self-control." *Current directions in psychological science* 16, no. 6 (2007): 351-355.

the muscles respond to resistance. Specifically, the capacity of the brain to exert self-control is limited but also expandable.

So a trip to the gym will be a struggle for the person whose muscles have sat idle. Naturally, they can expect to be unable to lift heavy, run fast, or last long. In the same way, someone who has not been paying any attention to establishing habits and routines in recent times will struggle when it is time to buckle down and try something new.

But if that couch potato keeps going to the gym and putting their muscles to work, you know what will happen. They will soon find that strength, speed, and stamina begin to adjust to the new demand. Well, Baumeister demonstrated that in the very same way, the more someone exerts their self-control, the more self-control they have at their disposal.

To demonstrate this phenomenon, one study compared two groups of participants: one that committed to a regular physical exercise regimen for two months and another group whose workout program was delayed until the experiment's conclusion. After these two months, both groups returned to the lab and were asked to complete one self-control task and then another, which under normal circumstances results in a significant dip in performance. Yet, only those who had not committed to the workout program showed the drop-off in performance typical of such experiments. And even though the tasks they were called on to perform were completely unrelated to physical fitness, the self-control of those who had consistently followed the workout plan held up; their performance showed almost no decline from the first task to the next.

Even more remarkable, those who had stayed committed to the exercise routine showed improved discipline in several everyday areas, including studying habits, substance use, emotional control, and even domestic routines like washing the dishes consistently. And before you write all this off as just the side effects of improved physical fitness, consider that the experiment was later repeated, substituting money management and study programs for exercise, again finding that those who had been "exercising" their self-control showed greater stamina on self-control tasks in the lab and improved discipline across domains in daily life.

By applying themselves and refusing to trade their self-interests for the fleeting interests of feelings and desires that lead back to square one, these individuals proved something to themselves. Maybe they learned to ignore the noise of resistance. Perhaps they heard the invitations to check out and said: "I'm sorry, but there is something I have to do." Whatever the case, the voice of determination started to call the shots in their lives, and they learned to stand firm in their commitments.

Action Items

It is called self-control because the self does not do what it ought to without the oversight of sound judgment. None of us are exempt from the tendency to be our own worst enemy if we pass off control to our feelings and desires. When we do that, we lie to ourselves about what we truly want and what we are truly capable of. We trade our ability to change ourselves and our circumstances for helplessness. Discipline is not easy, especially if you have not been exercising it. But here are some ways you can start:

1. **Your time is limited, and, as we have seen, so is your will-power.** These are your most precious resources. Be smart about how you invest them to ensure a meaningful return. Pick targets that align with your values and passions. These things will feed your self-respect and continue to inspire you as you watch them grow.

2. **Don't let yourself off the hook in establishing new routines and habits.** Also, remember that the endurance of your self-control is limited. Behavioral change researchers have

long recognized that trying to change everything at once is destined to fail. So, limit your endeavors to one or two to start. Before you know it, you might find yourself with a cabinet full of clean dishes.

3. **Fatigue, irritability, hunger, aches, and pains are all real adversaries that can make grand ideas fall by the wayside.** It is not necessary or even helpful to pretend those things don't exist but keep a healthy skepticism about what they encourage you to neglect. Committed action does not depend on the cooperation of your feelings, but it can often change them. Mood follows action.

The Not-So-Secret Ingredient to Success

As you know, those thousands of hours of training and miles of travel, months away from home, and less-than-ideal sleeping arrangements did not lead to the outcome I had been chasing for so long. Despite my commitment, I ultimately fell short of making it to the big leagues.

But one quality defined the whole journey: discipline. I had given my all to the path of my choosing, tuning out the desires that called me to check out, passing up the signs calling me to detour down the path of least resistance. I had learned to take my intentions seriously, keep the promises I made to myself, and treat the time I had available as a precious resource rather than an invitation to waste it. When my baseball career ended, the targets changed, but the principles that brought me there stayed the same. I had not become a major league baseball player, but I had become a professional.

As the story goes, I rediscovered my passion through real estate investing and eventually became a social media content creator. Text messaging sellers, contractors, and Realtors replaced batting and fielding reps. Scouting pitchers made way for reviewing housing specs. The crowd's roar for a game-winning home run turned into likes and shares on social media posts about the lessons I learned on the road to where I am today. And truth be told, my life now is a cakewalk compared to my time traveling the country playing baseball, using what little time I had leftover to stay afloat selling houses during a recession. But that time in the trenches forged a mindset of radical, unconditional commitment. No matter the game I choose to direct my commitment to, my success is no coincidence.

Today, I have scaled to the point where I have delegated many of the tasks I used to do to others, but that is because I reached a point where my talents and discipline were best served elsewhere. I have shifted my focus and leaned the ladder against a different wall I wake up to climb every day. One component of that focus is social media.

Sure, I get tired. Yes, it gets boring. Of course, I feel at a loss for ideas at times. Absolutely, I put hard work into the content I feel strongly about that gets criticized or, worse, ignored. None of those feelings, obstacles, and setbacks can touch the mental toughness I earned in the trenches when no one was around to make sure I showed up for me but me. What has remained unchanged through all the seasons of life, kept me anchored through the ups and the downs alike, is accountability to my own goals and values.

Everybody can do great when they feel great. But what about those who are consistent and prioritize what matters to them, regardless of how they feel? Those are the ones who find out what they are capable of. I have been more successful than 99 percent of those on social media because I stick to my routine and stand firm in my commitment when 99 percent of them take a day off. There is no magic formula to my success; there is only discipline.

CHAPTER 4

Quit the Comparison Game

"After so many years struggling to keep up with you,
I finally realized we're not even running the same race."

—SCOTT STABILE

Each Minor League Baseball team, from Single-A to Triple-A, is allotted between twenty-eight and thirty spots on their roster. By design, not a single player who occupies those few spots is content to remain there; all are competing, not only alongside teammates to defeat other teams but also as individuals striving to outperform *all* others and take a spot on the roster that represents the next step toward the majors.

Indeed, the game is built upon this cutthroat reality, where one man's fortune is another's misfortune. For nearly every home run, a pitcher missed his mark; for every strikeout, a batter swung and missed. At each step, there is a winner and a loser, a triumph and a tragedy. In a work environment where every man seeks to prove his best, competitiveness serves as the lifeblood of the game and the cardinal virtue of its participants.

It is also an environment ripe for envy. Paid pennies and fed scraps, all are fighting for the riches and feasts that await their graduation to the Major Leagues. And to move to the next tier of the minors, from Single-A to Double-A and Double-A to Triple-A, requires a spot to be open, a spot occupied by a person pursuing the same dream as you are. Naturally, then, players covet the spot of the person who plays their position at the next level, one step closer to the big leagues. For each aspirant, the odds are low, and the stakes are high.

It pains me to admit, but my desire to succeed in the minors existed alongside a desire for others to fail. Like everyone else, I wanted to advance, and as I saw it, that meant I needed the person above me to fail.

So I kept a close eye on my competition, scrambling daily to the stats page of the second baseman in the league above me, fingers crossed that they flubbed every grounder that came their way, whiffed at every pitch they were thrown, and, in my worst moments, twisted their ankle going down the dugout steps.

This was particularly true for players I did not like. To see them thriving felt like an injustice, like they were getting away with whatever quality earned them a spot on my crap list. They had what I wanted. They were in *my* spot, the one I deserved because of my hard work and virtue. Their flourishing was at my expense.

Of course, my competitiveness was not just a liability. My desire to win and be the best supercharged my effort, tenacity, and stubbornness in the face of adversity. But it was a weakness because, with a self-perception dependent upon being "the best," what happened when I lost? When your pride is built upon outdoing the other, and you lose, your whole persona crumbles.

Envy

Envy, according to researchers, arises when a person encounters a "similar other" who he or she perceives to enjoy superior quality, achievement, or possession in some area that is important to his or her view of the self.[9] Given that I took particular pride in my hitting abilities, envy might bubble up if I witnessed another minor league second baseman making plays that I questioned whether I could make. Of course, such a perceived discrepancy between self and seemingly-similar others also brings about a yearning to close that gap, to thrive in the ways that one sees the other thriving.

There are, however, two ways that envy manifests.[10] *Benign envy* occurs when the comparer perceives that they have some control over improving their performance in the area of discrepancy and that the object of comparison deserved or earned their favor. On the other hand, the person experiencing *malicious envy,* which is particularly common when the advantaged individual is disliked by the observer, believes there is little that they can do to close the gap and that the other is not deserving of what he or she has achieved.

The effects of each form of envy are predictable. Because the person who feels malignant envy holds to the belief that the other attained their advantages through no merit of their own, they also suppose that nothing can be done to attain them for themselves. Therefore, they find little reason to double down their effort to achieve the objects of their envy. Instead, they turn their attention toward the envied, wishing them failure or even harm.

---

9   Parrott, W. Gerrod, and Richard H. Smith. "Distinguishing the experiences of envy and jealousy." *Journal of personality and social psychology* 64, no. 6 (1993): 906.

10 Van de Ven, Niels, Marcel Zeelenberg, and Rik Pieters. "Leveling up and down: the experiences of benign and malicious envy." *Emotion* 9, no. 3 (2009): 419.

But individuals who do not question the deservingness of those they envy are much more likely to find the inspiration to work toward improvement. The thinking goes something like this: since that person who is similar to me earned their keep based on their merit, so can I.

Competition

Competitiveness is a trait inherent to most top performers. And when you imagine a very successful person, you will probably also envision someone who carries themselves with pride. But do you also see someone who pitches a fit when someone else does better than they do or achieves something they set out to achieve? Do you see someone who makes excuses, berates themselves, and throws their hands up when their efforts do not result in the outcome they had intended right away?

Proper competitiveness is founded upon striving—not winning. Competitiveness, wisely leveraged, aims to triumph, not over another individual, but over one's limitations. Proper pride is rooted in effort, where a person gives himself over to his or her gifts, talents, and potentialities. No one owes you anything, but you owe yourself your best.

Stanford psychologist Carol Dweck described a growth mindset as the belief that skills and abilities result from strategy and effort to learn.[11] Those with this mentality are not afraid of failing, but they are afraid of not trying. People with a growth mindset believe they can get smarter, better, and faster and that effort and persistence are the ingredients that make the difference. So they take challenges head-on, and they grow in the process. Like all others, sometimes they fail, sometimes they lose. But their response is what distinguishes them.

---

11 Dweck, Carol. "What having a 'growth mindset' actually means." *Harvard Business Review* 13, no. 2 (2016): 2-5.

In contrast, there are those who respond as though a failure like being outperformed by an opponent should not be a part of pursuing success. Moreover, they react defensively to feedback, treating it as though it were an attack on their ability. Essentially, they have an aversion to any indication that what they are doing and how they are doing it is not "right."

Looking back, I realize that I used to be this way sometimes. After a strike out or an error in the field, I often found myself lost in a profanity-laced tirade before catching myself and thinking: *What am I doing?* In those moments, all I saw was failure, not an opportunity to reflect on what had gone wrong and what I could do to address it and avoid the same mistake next time.

When you respond to a setback or negative feedback as though something is inherently wrong with you or that the task itself must be unfair, flawed, or impossible because you fell short of your intention, you have fallen into a "fixed mindset." Those with a growth mindset recognize adversity as a natural part of the endeavor. They are not only receptive to feedback, but they actively seek it out. They believe that learning and improvement happen when they strive for something and remain open to the lessons that accompany failure.

This is not just a mindset. This is the way things work.[12] There is no debate whether neural growth results from the actions we continually take, and the thoughts we continually think. Our brains and bodies are forever a work in progress, responding to the demands we place on them, correcting neural connections and muscle coordination to match the demands called to light by the mistakes made.

The equipment we work with is opportunistic, but we must provide the opportunities. Shy away from failure and feedback, and a fixed

---

12 Hiroyuli Okuno . Neuroplasticity. In D. Boison & S. A. Masino (Eds.), *Homeostatic control of brain function* (2016): 175–186.

mindset becomes a self-fulfilling prophecy. While one person belly-aches that they are not getting their expected outcome—that others are getting what *they* deserve—the person with a growth mindset is busy building and becoming.

Winning at All Costs

The mindset with which a person approaches competition plays a central role not only in their level of effort and resiliency in the face of adversity, but in the reason they compete, and how they go about it. Those with a growth mindset are likely to espouse *task-oriented goals*, seeking mastery of tasks such that competence is judged using the self as the standard. In other words, they judge their performance based on improvement. On the other hand, a fixed mindset is consistent with an *ego orientation*, where fulfillment is based not on effort and improvement but on demonstrating superior innate ability. The former focuses on improvement at the cost of effort; the latter focuses on winning at all costs.

Thus, ego orientation leaves a person's pride dependent upon an impossibility: perpetual superiority over all else. But that's not the only liability associated with this mindset. For those who base their fulfillment on demonstrating superiority to others, the focus on winning often overshadows integrity. In fact, studies have confirmed that those who subscribe to ego-oriented goals are likelier than the task-oriented to demonstrate poor sportsmanship, cheat, and endorse cheating as a valid path to victory.[13]

Those backhanded tactics might lead to victory, but the victory won through cheating fails to bring about the vindication of a win

---

13 Duda, Joan L., Linda K. Olson, and Thomas J. Templin. "The relationship of task and ego orientation to sportsmanship attitudes and the perceived legitimacy of injurious acts." *Research quarterly for exercise and sport* 62, no. 1 (1991): 79-87.

earned through fair play. Cheating deprives the victor of self-efficacy, the feeling that growth and mastery can be built through one's own capabilities and effort. In other words, the person who cheats to win is always left to wonder whether they could have done so on their own merit.

Whether in business or sports, if you sacrifice your integrity to win, you also forfeit the real, lasting satisfaction that comes from the win. That kind of satisfaction isn't threatened or taken away by the performance of another person, even one who did not follow the path of integrity. Winning at all costs fails when that cost is your own self-respect.

Action Items

Left unchecked, envy not only saps you of your drive and integrity but can also rob you of fulfillment in victory and learning in defeat. Below are a few ways to ensure that you don't play the losing game of defining yourself in comparison to others:

1. **Cultivate gratitude.** Research confirms that grateful people are less envious and more generous than those who are not. This makes sense. *Practices* of gratitude cultivate the *feelings* of gratitude by bringing our focus to what we have, which is incompatible with dwelling on what we lack. One such practice (which I do every morning) is to simply make a habit of writing down the things you are grateful for. This simple practice has demonstrated benefits that extend far beyond reduced envy, including improved sleep, reduced symptoms of illness, and more happiness.

2. **Check your social media consumption.** Whereas we may have compared ourselves in the past to those in our immediate vicinity, our objects of comparison through social media are endless. Not only that but what we typically see is the very best of their lifestyle. Be accountable to yourself when scrolling social media

and, to the greatest extent possible, filter accounts and content you cannot honestly say are contributing to your growth. Mindless scrolling not only takes up time for the sake of "entertainment," but that entertainment may also come at the cost of your own contentment with what you have compared to the very best of what others are willing to show you.

3. **Give generously.** I already mentioned that grateful people are less envious and more generous than those who are not. Well, it follows that the generous people also tend to be less envious and more grateful. Give to a cause. Celebrate the achievements of a person who might otherwise incite your envy through praise or congratulations. As you'll see in the next chapter, there are many ways to live with generosity.

The Only Comparison That Matters

"This is the pre-boarding announcement for flight 28C to Orlando. We would like to invite our first-class customers to begin the boarding process," the gate agent announced.

The days of traveling city to city by bus were a distant memory as I extended the handle of my Louis Vuitton bag and weaved through the feet of passengers who would soon walk past me and through the curtain to the rear of the plane.

It was 2020, seven years into my house-flipping journey, and I was headed to Florida for an invitation-only mastermind group for over 200 of the country's most prolific real estate investors. For those unfamiliar, a mastermind group is one where people regularly gather together with a mutual commitment to growth in their chosen field. Attendees share two common and reciprocal purposes: to ask for and offer help. This particular mastermind was for the best of the best in real estate, the first class. In other words, my invitation meant I was a big dog, and I had happily paid the twenty-five grand required to punch my ticket to attend.

But all of my perceived status melted away when I arrived at the event. This "big dog" was just average when surrounded by a list of attendees who averaged more than a hundred deals a year. No one would bat an eye at the size of my portfolio. No one would be impressed or envious of my LV bag. These were the big hitters, many whose enormous successes dwarfed what I had achieved to that point.

But in this setting, there was no place for ego. There was no competition against the other for a spot at the next level. Sure, I felt some envy for those who had reached heights that I aspired to. But whereas years ago I kept a close watch on my competition in hopes that they might blow the opportunity that would clear the way for mine, at that mastermind, I watched and listened closely for the ideas and inspiration that might bring me closer to the fulfillment of my goals and aspirations. I realized that regardless of how far we had come in our personal and professional journeys to this point, we were all assembled here unified in competition against a single, undefeated opponent: our unrealized potential.

I was further reminded of the absurdity of comparison when I got the opportunity to deliver a presentation to my fellow attendees about the emerging influence of blockchain on the real estate industry. After an hour of discussing ways my audience could expect the digital, decentralized forms of currency like Bitcoin to change the nature of real estate transactions, I opened the floor for questions.

Given my reverence for my fellow attendees and, in some ways, my inflated perception of their competence, I was caught off guard by the first question asked. "Okay, that all sounds great," a man in the second row conceded, "but I have a question. What is blockchain?" From the laughter and nods of agreement that followed, I realized that this audience, made up of the savviest investors in the country, didn't know the first thing about these new frontiers. I also realized the inroad I had in the real estate game (which most of my colleagues were completely ignorant of), which would later lead me to create my own mastermind. It would be a mastermind for those interested in digital real estate who could learn the fundamentals and gather to build together, invest together, and continually stay at the cutting edge of this emerging market.

I arrived in Florida as a big fish who had left his pond and returned home humbled by the realization that there are plenty in the sea who are just as big and often much bigger. I also departed with a deepened appreciation for the futility of comparison based on "size" when everyone's criteria for success differs. In the words quoted to begin this chapter: "I finally realized we're not even running the same race."

I had listened to my fellow attendees' struggles and triumphs. I had shared my own. I had offered insights when I saw that I could be of service and learned from the wisdom shared by those who had traveled my path. And thanks to all of this, both the giving and receiving, I returned home inspired, with renewed clarity on the race I was running and the contribution I could make. I returned knowing that the only valid comparison was the one between my actual and ideal self and feeling renewed in my determination to make them one and the same.

CHAPTER 5

The Law of Reciprocity

"Service to others is the rent you pay for your room here on Earth."

—MUHAMMAD ALI

Once I got my foot in the door and a little momentum on my side in the house-flipping game, I began regularly attending a Las Vegas real estate meetup to network and learn from the successes and setbacks of others sharing the playing field of real estate with me. In 2015 at one of those meetings, I spotted a guy I would later come to know as Mike.

During that time, I still grabbed a used couch now and again when I spotted a deal that I knew would bring in some extra cash, and it was Mike who one day arrived at my storage unit to buy one such couch I had on hand. I immediately recognized him from the Vegas meetings and soon found out he was actively flipping mobile homes in the Vegas real estate market. It wasn't long before a conversation about business turned to talk of God and faith, and before I knew it, Mike had invited me to attend a Bible study, something I had never done before.

Rewind to a few months earlier, when I struck up a friendship with a guy at my church named John. We quickly bonded over our shared desire to grow in faith and love of pickup basketball. Over the coming months, our relationship remained at that level of familiarity, split between encounters at church and the occasional arrangement to meet up and shoot some hoops.

Well, the day came for my first Bible study, and when I showed up at the address Mike had given me, lo and behold, it turned out to be the home of my basketball buddy, John. At the time, this seemed like nothing more than an amusing coincidence and a welcome relief to me as the lone newcomer to the Bible study. In no way did I anticipate the grace of that moment and the massive impact it would come to have on the trajectory of my life.

The Spark of Generosity

During our time in that Bible study, the relationship between John and I grew far beyond a shared enjoyment of basketball to the mutual sharing of the most intimate details of our lives. Through our weekly meetings and the time we began to spend together outside the group, we developed mutual regard and trust for one another. As such, John was aware of what I was doing in house-flipping and, like the other group members, was always there to hear me out and offer encouragement through the ups and downs of my newfound career.

But over a round of golf with John, the chance meeting at his house a year prior would come full circle to a moment that would completely alter the trajectory of my career and life. Despite never having once asked John for money, he suddenly turned to me and said, "Ryan, I want to invest a couple hundred thousand dollars in what you're doing and just see where it goes." No paperwork, no contract, and no conditions. John wagered his money on a conviction that I would be a good steward of his generosity, and he left the fruits of that investment to his faith in me and in what he felt Jesus was calling him to do.

I was taken aback, overcome with gratitude, and humbled by his trust in me—and I was also determined. John had handed over his money to me without condition, and I fully intended to repay his generosity and express my gratitude through my wholehearted commitment to ensuring that he did not regret his faith in me and my vision.

The Getting in Giving

A long-standing theory of generosity tries to reconcile the commonality of generosity with general assumptions of human selfishness. Over time, researchers in this camp attempted to come up with reasons a person would act in seemingly selfless ways by theorizing answers to the hypothetical question posed by the giver, "What's in it for me?" They concluded that people must act generously to improve their reputations, get on another's good side, or have their generosity reciprocated.

A 2011 study questioned everything, including the fundamental premise that humans are selfish.[14] In the study, participants were hooked up to a brain scanner while they played a game in which they were asked to divide resources between themselves and others. The choice of how much to share was theirs, and there was no possibility that they would experience the social consequences that theorists had proposed as the deterrents to stinginess and catalysts to generosity—withholding wouldn't damage their reputation, draw the ire of the person denied, or make it less likely they might be treated

14 Zaki, Jamil, and Jason P. Mitchell. "Equitable decision making is associated with neural markers of intrinsic value." *Proceedings of the National Academy of Sciences* 108, no. 49 (2011): 19761-19766.

generously. Yet even without those possibilities, participants shared more than was required.

More interesting were the brain scan results. When participants gave more than was necessary and acted more generously, there was increased activation in the brain's reward center, the same part that lights up when a person takes a bite of chocolate, for example. On the other hand, when participants kept most of the money and therefore withheld more from the other, a part of the brain associated with negative emotions like pain and disgust was activated.

Findings from another study that explored whether there are exceptions to the old adage, "Money can't buy happiness," painted a similar picture. They found that the happiness people experienced as a result of spending money on others actually exceeded the money they spent on themselves.[15]

So what does this all mean? It means that acting generously *feels* good. It means that we are not inherently selfish and, in fact, take satisfaction from the act of giving. And it means that the gift really *is* in the giving.

The Greatest Gift

When most people think of generosity, they think of giving money, and money is certainly a part of it. But generosity extends far beyond the financial. Perhaps the one resource that best embodies the spirit of generosity is the gift that can't be reclaimed, through repayment or redoubling of effort to earn it back. The most precious gift is a person's time.

---

15 Dunn, Elizabeth W., Lara B. Aknin, and Michael I. Norton. "Prosocial spending and happiness: Using money to benefit others pays off." *Current directions in psychological science* 23, no. 1 (2014): 41-47.

Through acts of service, we offer our time, energy, and presence for the betterment of another individual. Acts as simple as bringing coffee to your spouse or stopping to help a stranded person on the side of the road can go a long way toward making another feel valued and reaping the benefits that come through the act of giving.

We serve when we take the time to listen to a person in need and offer them empathy, encouragement, and feedback for what they are going through. This type of generosity plays a central role in mentorship, which has contributed massively to my success. Through close listening and direct feedback about my unique personal and professional issues, mentorship has represented quite possibly the most powerful source of my education and development as a man and a professional.

Education is another means by which a person can extend the generosity of their time and perhaps the one I practice most often. We all possess unique skills and knowledge that can benefit others. Anything of value in your life represents an opportunity for generosity toward another. Social media offers an ideal medium for sharing information quickly and widely that could save others a great deal of time, effort, and struggle they might go through without the knowledge you have learned through your own experience.

Of course, we are all busy, but that is precisely why the gifts of time can have such an impact on the giver and the receiver. It requires that we stop and offer the full gift of our presence to another person, and it's through our presence that we demonstrate and affirm to another that they are valued.

Scarcity and Abundance

When you hold a scarcity mindset, you believe there is not enough to go around for everyone. There's not enough time, not enough money, not enough business, not enough food, not enough happiness, not enough anything, and this perception of lack produces fear that you won't get your share. Such a perspective offers a compelling argument for hoarding. When there's not enough to go around, you had better keep a grip on what you have and tell no one where you found it or how to get it.

On the other hand, a person with an abundance mindset believes that life is bountiful and generative. A person with this mentality meets apparent limitations with creativity instead of despair. They always think of what can be done rather than getting stuck on what's not possible. Behind generosity is a belief in abundance and interdependence; there is plenty to go around, and what's good for you is good for me.

And yet, you can't always rely on feelings to precede action. Just as an abundance mindset brings about acts of generosity, acts of generosity can inspire the development of an abundance mindset. Perhaps the best way to discover abundance is through giving and recognizing the opportunities that arise from generosity. It works like this: the hand that is open to giving is also open to receiving. Giving relieves you of the need to hold on.

This applies not only to material abundance but to the satisfaction you get in return for giving. The examples are, well, abundant. Couples who perform acts of kindness and sacrifice for one another report greater relationship satisfaction and less likelihood of divorce.[16] Those who work where prosocial behaviors are promoted and practiced are more motivated and creative.[17] Even physical health is more abundant among those who give—those who give more generously

---

16 Dew, Jeffrey, and W. Bradford Wilcox. "Give and You Shall Receive? Generosity, Sacrifice, & Marital Quality." (2011).

17 Grant, Adam M., and Justin M. Berg. "Prosocial motivation at work." In *The Oxford handbook of positive organizational scholarship*. 2011.

live longer, have lower blood pressure, and get better sleep. They even hear better![18]

Popular culture emphasizes focusing on yourself; indeed, part of being a useful adult is being responsible for your own care. Nevertheless, we're discovering that one of the best ways to care for the self is through caring for others. Too much effort is squandered when people try to outdo others, go it alone, and keep all the wealth and all the power to themselves when the reality is, we elevate ourselves from the inside out by elevating others.

Action Items

We've seen the many benefits that accompany the act of giving. Here are some of the actions you can take now to begin cultivating generosity in your life:

1. **Choose a charity and give.** As we've seen, giving contributes to your mood, it increases your life satisfaction, it is beneficial to your health, and of course, it eases the burden of the person you are donating to. It's also important to donate to a cause that aligns with your values, producing even stronger motivation for your giving.

2. **Budget for giving.** The Bible says in 2 Corinthians 9:7, "Each of you should give what you have decided in your heart to give." These are wise words—research confirms that those who give under compulsion enjoy none of the many benefits enjoyed by eager givers.

3. **Join a social group or organization centered around volunteering.** There are many individual opportunities for volun-

---

18 Allen, Summer. "The science of generosity." *A white paper prepared for the John Templeton Foundation by the Greater Good Science Center at UC Berkeley* (2018).

teering, but doing so within a social setting may foster a sense of community and incorporate an additional element of social connection to the act of volunteering. Meetup.com and Facebook groups are examples of where you might find this type of group. You might also consider a local church to point you toward available volunteer opportunities.

The Fruits of Generosity

John put his money on the line because he believed in my character, inspiring me to live up to his view of my character and potential. The friendship we developed in a year of Bible study and through his investment in me, both personal and financial, led to a deep and mutual commitment, first to our faith in God and each other, and second to business. His investment in me took me to heights I had never imagined at the time. Fate was on our side.

John's initial leap of faith in me resulted in a successful outcome that further grew his faith in me and strengthened the conviction that first led him to offer his partnership. In the coming months, a couple hundred thousand dollars turned into half a million, which soon became over a million. Eventually, he told his friends, and the spark that started with a chance meeting at church spread to expand and scale my business like wildfire.

I now look back and believe that God orchestrated a chain of events that led me to a deep connection with a person who would believe in my character and invest in my vision, jumpstart my business, and put me in a position where my potential would be so much higher, my reach so much farther, and my opportunity to pay forward the generosity that John showed me so much greater.

My success and wealth exceeded what I dared to even dream of when I started in real estate thanks in no small part to the generosity of people like John. Along with it came the even greater fortune that

Mindy and I enjoy in our ability to give to others in the same way. There's no wealth more gratifying and pure than that which we reap through caring for others.

Are you willing to help someone else?

I hope you've benefited from what you've read so far. Do you think others would benefit from reading it as well? If so, I have a big ask of you...

Would you go to Amazon and leave a review on this book? It doesn't cost you anything other than a few minutes of your time. It's simple to do on your phone or Kindle.

Once again, it only takes a few minutes of your time, but it could change the trajectory of someone's entire life.

As a thank you for your support, I am offering you *free access to the "Business Builder Academy"*, the step-by-step framework I used to build seven million-dollar businesses from the ground up. You can access it by submitting a screenshot of your review below.

↓

WEALTHYWAY.COM/REVIEW

PART II

Action

CHAPTER 6

You Don't Get More Time

"Efficiency is doing things right;
effectiveness is doing the right things."

—PETER DRUCKER

My time to make a difference starts when the alarm sounds. It's early, 6:00 a.m., but I was in bed reading by ten and asleep by eleven, so I'm well-rested. I won't head to the office for another four hours, which leaves me plenty of time to invest in myself before the busyness of the day takes hold.

I head straight to the shower and step out with a fresh mind. By 6:30 a.m., I'm dressed and making a pre-workout drink, an old habit from my baseball days. From there, I turn my morning and my attention over to God. I pray, read my Bible, and finish feeling mentally and spiritually equipped for the day. I do these before everything that comes after because they represent what's most important to me and the foundation of all that's to come, my relationship with Jesus.

From there, I open my Wealthy Way Planner, which I'll cover in chapter nine. This contains my journal, gratitude list, and weekly and yearly goals. It serves as a system of accountability to myself since I can clearly see a running tally of my progress on the year and whether I stuck to the commitments I made to myself yesterday. It tells me whether I need to stay the course or correct it.

By then, I'm ready to put that pre-workout drink to work. Is it better to work out in the morning? At night? I don't know, but what I do know is that a good workout is a done workout, and I know I am far more likely to talk myself out of a workout at the end of the workday when I am tired and want to go home to see my wife and kids. So I get it done, and afterward, I feel accomplished and mentally sharp.

Finally, I go home, eat breakfast, and shower *again* (this time to couple my fresh mind with fresh pits). Having attended to my core needs, I finally turn my service outward. My mind and conscience are clear, and it's time to go to work.

The Morning Routine

Most start their day in reactive mode. The alarm goes off as late as possible, leaving just enough time to shower, brush their teeth, fill up their to-go cup, and head off to the grind, not to what they want to do, but what they "have" to do. They do the bare minimum that will get them to the place they have to be by the time they have to be there to accomplish the things they have to accomplish. No wonder a little extra sleep offers the main consolation to facing this thankless reality day after day.

The alternative is to establish a morning routine. The idea is to be proactive versus reactive, not scrolling through social media, not waking up with so little time that you have to run around like your hair is on fire, but starting your day with a win that gets you mentally, physically, and spiritually ahead.

Morning is a reset, *your* reset. Those who wake to urgency and compulsion are bound to repeat yesterday's mistakes. But a morning begun with intention can offer the opportunity to reflect on the state of your conscience relative to the values you wish to embody. If you had a bad day yesterday or a bad run of late, it is the time to redirect and recommit to a plan that will move you to a place you will feel proud of and excited about.

My morning routine serves as the time to nourish the values I will carry through my day and into my interactions with the people on my team, whether that be family, friends, or coworkers. The emphasis is on those aspects of myself that transcend my work and serve as the foundation and the reason for everything else I do, namely, my faith and relationship with Jesus. As such, I begin my morning routine with the Bible and prayer, which serve to ground and humble me before God and prepare me to bring an attitude of gratitude and service into everything I do.

For others, maybe it's some other inspirational book and meditation. The point is to fill yourself with positive energy and purpose. Your morning routine should remind you of what matters so that you kick off your day on steady ground and with clear direction.

Every Day I'm Hustlin'

There is an unfortunate trend among entrepreneurs, real estate investors, and beyond to wear the number of hours worked as a badge of honor. Those who subscribe to "hustle culture" act as though their entire identity is founded upon outworking everyone else. But a person who brags about working eighty-hour weeks unwittingly confesses their stupidity. The attention span does not last that long. The gas tank does not have that capacity. An eighty-hour work week is a surefire prescription for inefficiency at best and burnout at worst.

Typically, these people are either lying to prop up their egos or giving themselves far too many hours to complete what could be done in a fraction of the time. When I am out spending time with my family, working on my health, or playing golf, these guys are dillydallying and calling it "hustle." They are like the gym rats who gloat about their three-hour workout; the workout where they chatted for an hour, paced in front of the mirror for ninety minutes and squeezed in a few sets and loud grunts somewhere in the thirty minutes in between.

Working twelve-hour days and neglecting health, hobbies, relationships, and everything else that's not "work" isn't cool. Sleep deprivation is not cool. It's a complete failure of priorities and self-respect.

Time Management Is Life Management

How you spend your time and where you choose to direct your attention is "life." Time management is the principle above all others, the canvas on which you paint your masterpiece. Time is your most precious resource, non-renewable and non-refundable.

Lose your money, and you can make it back. Yet, once you have failed to seize the opportunity of *this* moment, you have lost your chance. And this moment, the one you are in now? It's the only one guaranteed and the only one you'll ever be able to do anything about. Do not take it for granted. Do not depend on taking advantage of unguaranteed time. Take advantage of the one that is. Do not take advantage of life.

Two principles frame time as the precious resource that it is: the Pareto Principle and Parkinson's Law.

Pareto's Principle

In 1895, Italian economist Vilfredo Pareto noticed that 80 percent of the land was owned by 20 percent of the population.[19] As unique a phenomenon as this initially seemed, he soon began to notice that this

---

19 Vilfredo Pareto, *Manuale di Econimia Politica* (Milano: Societa Editrice, 1906).

input-output ratio held in all manner of phenomenon. He noticed, for example, that the principle held even in his own garden, where 80 percent of his pea pods came from 20 percent of his plants.

Eventually, this principle found its way into the business world when Joseph Juran, a management consultant for General Motors, began to question whether it was even more universal than Pareto had realized. In business, he started to see it pop up everywhere. For example, he discovered that 80 percent of the production defects resulted from only 20 percent of the causes. Many years later, Microsoft found that the same percentages of bugs were responsible for 80 percent of its errors and crashes.

So as it goes, the principle was settled as follows: just 20 percent of causes lead to 80 percent of the results, whether favorable or unfavorable. And as it applies to time management, the Pareto Principle goes like this: 20 percent of what you do produces 80 percent of the results you get.

For busy entrepreneurs, this principle is absolutely crucial. In the days of Pareto, the 20 percent who held the 80 percent had access to the same number of hours each day as the rest of the population. And yet somehow, they were leveraging those hours more effectively. Presumably, they were focusing their time and efforts on actions that led to exponentially greater results.

So how does the Pareto Principle apply when you sit down with your to-do list? Well, the same people that wake to the singular urgent task of getting to work on time tend to carry that mindset throughout their day, focusing on the urgent and unprofitable at the expense of the important and impactful. Instead, they should start with the actions more likely to produce the greatest return, whether that relates to finances or well-being. Whenever possible, tasks that are mindless and necessary only to keep you afloat ought to be delegated, but

more on that in chapter eight. For now, ask yourself these questions to
determine what tasks deserve your time and attention:

- What are the most important projects for me now,
considering my values and goals?

- Which of my products accounts for the majority of my sales?

- Am I leveraging my strengths in what I'm doing, or can
this be delegated?

- What time of day am I most productive?

- What are the 20 percent of activities that are creating
80 percent of my distraction?

- What activities in my personal life produce the
most happiness?

With those questions answered, you should have a more reasonable idea of your priorities. Now you just have to manage the time
allotted for their execution.

Parkinson's Law

When Microsoft Japan implemented a four-day workweek in 2019,
something weird happened. Despite having 20 percent less time to
complete their work, productivity increased by 40 percent.[20] Time-
wasting and fatigue gave way to focus and efficiency, and Microsoft's
seeming generosity paid dividends.

Pareto's Principle suggests you can achieve most of your results
with a few things you do. Parkinson's law states that the amount of
time it will take to complete those few things will drag on for as long

20 Bill Chappell, "4-Day Workweek Boosted Workers' Productivity By 40%, Microsoft Japan
Says," NPR, November 4, 2019, https://www.npr.org/2019/11/04/776163853/microsoft-
japan-says-4-day-workweek-boosted-workers-productivity-by-40.

as the time you allot for their completion.[21] This is the dirty secret behind the claims of the hustler who "works" twelve hours a day and the gym rat who "works out" for three.

Pareto's Principle suggests that we will drag out the completion of our tasks as long as possible, so we must combat that tendency. The solution is to define the tasks to be completed clearly and the time available to do them firmly. Deadlines keep us honest and accountable to a self-set standard.

Princeton behavioral scientist Elder Shafir explained the effectiveness of deadlines like this: "When you have a deadline it's like a storm ahead of you or having a truck around the corner. It's menacing and it's approaching, so you focus heavily on the task."[22] Of course, there is an odd tendency for most to treat the deadlines we set for ourselves as less important than those set by others. There are a couple of ways to deal with this tendency.

One is to broadcast your deadline for others to hear and know. That way, if you go against your word to yourself, it won't just be you that knows. In other words, leverage the power of shame.

The other is to remind yourself what's at stake for making and breaking a commitment to yourself. Let's say you've ensured another person that you will have something important to them done at a particular time. What do you fear will happen if you break that commitment? What happens when you leave your friend stranded at the airport when you promised you'd be there to pick them up? What is the cost of forgetting to send over that research your boss asked that you have ready for the presentation he'll give first thing tomorrow? Maybe you're afraid they'll lose respect for you. Perhaps you fear that

---

21 Cyril Parkinson, *Parkinson's Law: Or the Pursuit of Progress*, (London: J. Murray, 1958).

22 Tiffanie Wen, "The 'Law; That Explains Why You Can't Get Anything Done," BBC, May 21, 2020, https://www.bbc.com/worklife/article/20191107-the-law-that-explains-why-you-cant-get-anything-done/.

they'll come to see you as unreliable and lose faith that you'll keep your commitments in the future. Or maybe, they'll lose their desire to share your company altogether.

Well, what do you think happens subconsciously when you commit to buckle down and get something that you have deemed important to you done in a certain amount of time and time and again end up blowing it off instead? Let's say you're unhappy with your health, decide that you need to start exercising, then watch days pass without the decision translating to action. Let's face it: your inaction suggests that you don't see yourself as worth the effort. When you break an agreement with yourself, you do so at the cost of your self-respect.

Action Items

Time management is about accomplishing the most impactful things in the least amount of time so that you have the time left to invest in the most important things. Here are a few of the ways that you can avoid spinning your wheels on your way to where you're going:

1. **Order your to-do list based on Pareto's Principle.** What activities will produce the most results relative to the effort required? Do those first. What will make the most profit, whether that be financial or otherwise? Consider, too, those few things that cause the most distractions. If certain items do not align with your strengths or someone else is more qualified, consider delegating.

2. **Schedule your most challenging tasks when your energy is highest and arrange your environment for minimal distraction.** According to Harvard Business School professor Teresa Amabile, it can take nineteen minutes to refocus on a task when

distracted.[23] So turn off notifications, avoid your phone and email, work far away from chatty officemates, and throw your phone out the window if necessary.

3. **Don't neglect free time for money.** One study demonstrated that those who gave up more money in favor of getting back free time ended up experiencing more joy and satisfaction in their lives and more fulfillment in their careers and social relationships. Maybe the best investment of your money is an investment in free time through outsourcing and delegation, a topic we will cover in chapter eight.

Buy Time

My morning routine culminates in the scheduling of my day, and I schedule my day on the same basis that I live out my mornings–based on my values. I determine where to invest my limited time and energy based on the life I want to live and the person I want to become.

- How much do I want to work?
- How much do I want to sleep?
- When do I want to work out?
- When do I want to hang out with my family and my friends?

My answers to questions like these are the raw materials of my schedule. It is as simple as that. I plan my time to ensure that none of the areas of life that I value are neglected so that I can appreciate and enjoy my work. It is why I excel at my various "jobs" because work is not everything I do. Work is not happening at the expense of everything else; it is not taking away from those things. I never think, "If I

---

23 Dina Gerdemen, "Want to Be Happier? Make More Free Time," Harvard Business School, October 5, 2020, https://hbswk.hbs.edu/item/want-to-be-happier-make-more-free-time/.

finish my work, then I will…" Those are no less important than work and no less a priority.

For most of my professional life, I have gone to work at ten and left at five, Monday through Friday. Recently, I have streamlined even further, working Monday through Thursday and golfing on Friday without any apparent drop-off in productivity. This is thanks to applying the principles taught by Pareto and Parkinson, principles that have only become more relevant and crucial in today's world, where options and information are endless.

I don't work on weekends. I give myself a lot of tasks to accomplish in the span of those four days and twenty-eight hours. I know I have limited time, that every one of those twenty-eight hours is precious, so I have to make the most of them. In fact, I would be willing to bet that, like the Microsoft workers in Japan, I get more done in that time than the "hustlers" who work eighty-hour weeks.

In the time left over, I ensure that each of the six areas of my life, which I cover in part three of this book, aren't neglected. I plan to ensure that my priorities are prioritized as reflected in my actions, not just my intentions. I plan to have no regrets.

If you are living a reactionary lifestyle, waking to urgency, and working just to get to the end of the day, you are leaving the things you hope to experience to factors beyond your control. You are always waiting for circumstances to be different so that it will be easier to make the things happen that you want to happen. In reality, that is a delusion. You don't get more time; you have to make it.

You are in the driver's seat when you sit down with your schedule. How do you want to live? That is the question when you sit down and plan your day. Reactive or responsible? Yes, there are only twenty-four hours in the day. All that means is that you had better be sure to make the most of each and every one.

CHAPTER 7

Embrace the Power of Solitude

"Solitude is the furnace of transformation.
Without solitude we remain victims of our society and
continue to be entangled in the illusions of the false self."

—HENRI NOUWEN

True solitude is rare these days. There is always a running monologue drowning out your thoughts. Some reading this may say: "Well, I have no issue at all with being alone." But how often are you *really* alone when you withdraw from whatever you use to entertain and distract you from being with your thoughts? Do you check social media? Listen to the radio? Muffle your sorrows with the noise coming from your TV? You get it. You are rarely ever *truly* alone.

In chapter one, we talked about fear of the unknown and the fact that so many avoid risks because they prefer the safety of their status quo, no matter how bland or unpleasant that status quo may be. This is just as relevant to your inner world as to the outside world. Many are so accustomed to filling every moment with noise—YouTube, gaming, Netflix, social media—that they actually fear getting quiet and still because of what they might find there. So they compensate. They default to the familiar and predictable to fill the space. Or they fall prey to the predictable novelty of algorithms that show users precisely the videos, posts, and products that will snatch their attention when they log on to a particular social account—*We noticed you like puppies. Well, wait until you see the video we have for you!* Being alone and actually paying attention to yourself isn't always comfortable, especially if it's not something you often do. Besides, there are plenty of options, and videos of adorable puppies, right at your fingertips to rescue you when discomfort starts to surface.

Much of part one of this book involved discussions about the importance of taking action, about acting upon the external world with faith and decisiveness. But as we began to see in the last chapter, wise and profitable action in the external world starts with familiarity with our internal world.

In solitude, we come to recognize what paths align with our deeply held values—the same ones that will ultimately bring about not just financial wealth but the wealth of the mind and spirit. Without time alone to take inventory of your strengths and weaknesses, victories and failures, you are at risk of drifting aimlessly or aiming at something that won't even bring fulfillment if you hit it by chance.

Along with that direction, time alone provides the time and space to check in with yourself to evaluate where you stand relative to those places you have decided are yours to pursue. Sure, you can check your bank account and assets, your followers, and the comments and likes they're leaving. But are you checking in on the things that aren't so easily quantified? Are you checking in on the state of your conscience? Your self-respect? Are you checking in on whether all of your efforts are leading you somewhere you want to go? Whether all that money, all those followers are leading to fulfillment?

Taking time out to be in your own presence is an antidote to living reactively, to waking up to the crisis of another day until you get through your "have-to" list so you can tune out again. It takes time, space, and intention to look at the reality of your situation and know how to wisely respond. That includes not wallowing in our mistakes but looking at them clearly so they can be corrected to create new consequences. It means asking: What could I have done differently? What lessons can I take from this event, this season of life?

The Social Media Slot Machine

The Las Vegas casino industry brings in thirteen billion dollars annually, equaling about thirty-six million daily. You don't need to be a mathematician to realize that they are playing a winning game against those who choose to try their luck and lay down their bets. If you asked the gamblers, one by one, who they believed netted more profits between the gamblers and the casinos, I doubt many would guess that the casino owners willingly took a loss out of generosity toward their guests or desperation that they may eventually turn the odds in their favor. But that doesn't stop 74 percent of the forty-two million annual visitors to Las Vegas who walk into the casinos like pigs to the slaughter.[24]

Now picture the line of gamblers at Caesars Palace, hands gripping the slot machine lever, glazed eyes fixed on the neon displays illuminating their dazed faces. And the next time you arrive a bit early at your gate at the airport, look at the line of fellow passengers waiting to board, thumbs hovering over smartphone screens, caught in an endless loop of *swipe, swipe*—switch apps—*swipe* again. Both

---

24 Will Yacowitz, "Nevada Hits All-Time Record of $13.4 Billion in Gambling Revenue in 2021," *Forbes,* January 27, 2022, https://www.forbes.com/sites/willyakowicz/2022/01/27/nevada-hits-all-time-record-of-134-billion-in-gambling-revenue-in-2021/?sh=175a70b-168bc/.

are refreshing and scanning, unsure when the next burst of endorphins will come, but sure that if they keep tugging and swiping away, it eventually will.

That is the sinister magic of what psychologists call "intermittent reinforcement."[25] Rewards delivered at irregular intervals will lead rational people to act pretty irrationally. If you needed a reminder of how dumb we can be, this phenomenon was first discovered with lab rats that worked harder and longer to get a crumb that came unpredictably than the ones they had direct and immediate control over.

Now, it would be pretty hypocritical for me to suggest you avoid things like social media and YouTube altogether. What I do suggest is that you not leave your consumption to chance. Don't open those apps and visit those sites mindlessly, swiping and scanning for some sugary treat served on a silver platter to stuff into your brain. Instead, consume your content the same way I create it—with a purpose. YouTube and Instagram are no more interested in the growth of your character than the casinos are in the growth of your bank account.

Don't make the mistake I did in my twenties and choose your learning resources strictly based on what's free and readily available on the internet (more on that in chapter eleven.) Instead, during your downtime, consume only what you truly believe will contribute to your growth. If you're clicking in search of a jolt of excitement, you'll eventually find it. But rest assured that, before long, you'll be just another sucker that's fallen for the sinister magic of intermittent reinforcement, pressing and swiping that screen like a rat trying to get a crumb.

---

25 B.F. Skinner, B. F. (1956). "A case history in scientific method," *American Psychologist*, 11(5), 221-233.

Journaling

What has been happening in your life recently? Tell me about yesterday. What went well, and what are you proud of? What did you screw up royally, and what could you have done differently? It seems like there's something on your mind. What is bothering you? There are things you might say to a spouse, a friend, a sibling, or maybe a coworker. They're questions that, when asked of you, give you an opportunity to step back and reflect. They're the ones that leave you feeling cleansed or freshly determined once you've gotten the answers out of your conscience and off your chest. They're also the kind that most people rarely bother asking themselves.

That's where journaling comes in. Journaling is about making the time and the space to confide in yourself. It gives you permission to share your disappointments, dreams, potentialities, limitations, and where you stand relative to those things without reservation. Journaling gives your mind the space and the attention to propose new thoughts and ideas, to talk about things you want to do and accomplish. We get so busy and distracted that the sounding board is completely drowned out. We never bother to ask ourselves how it's going. We never even bother asking whether the things we're doing are worth the time they're eating up. When we're not making the time and the space to confide those things in ourselves, we can easily find that we're living on auto-pilot, not even steering the ship.

For many of you, journaling may sound like a chore, like having an essay assigned every day of the week. That makes sense. Take a couple of months off from working out, and see how exciting a trip to the track or the gym sounds. But the feelings of aversion to journaling are just as misleading as the ones that tell you that getting off your butt won't be worth it.

Did you know that people who keep a diary recording the things they are stressed out about experience less depression, anxiety, and hostility than those who do not? And what if I told you that regu-lar journaling boosts the immune system, that even a short season of writing down thoughts and feelings has been shown to result in fewer doctor visits and even reduces symptoms of chronic diseases like asthma and arthritis?[26] Does that ten-minute, self-assigned essay still seem like a waste of your time?

No matter how tough you claim to be, the fact is that stuffing down your emotions is terrible for your health. And you don't have to be a psychologist to know that anxiety and worry aren't going to help you work efficiently on that thing that can't wait an extra fif-teen minutes for you to get started on; gnawing worry eats away at mental energy that could be applied to creative solutions, and it can take all of that energy just to get out of bed when you're depressed. Additionally, plowing ahead without taking stock of how things are going is a recipe for futility and frustration. But then again, you'll get to tell yourself that you're tough and don't need it, and that's what really matters, right?

Content Creation: Journaling in Public

Journaling provides a proven and powerful means of knowing your-self, and social media gets in the way, right? Not necessarily. Apps and websites like YouTube, Instagram, and TikTok are ready-made for documenting your journey. In many ways, they make an ideal reposi-tory for your process and the trajectory of your growth. Documenting online what's happening in your life and business can offer the same opportunity to get clear and honest with yourself about where you stand on this leg of your journey as much as writing in your journal.

---

26 Kira M. Newman, "How Journaling Can Help You Through Hard Times," *Greater Good Magazine,* August 18, 2020, https://greatergood.berkeley.edu/article/item/how_journaling_can_help_you_in_hard_times/.

The beauty of using social media as a means of journaling your path is that it has the potential to benefit the creator and others as your audience. You might ask, "But what if I'm new to what I'm doing? I'm not an expert, so why would anyone listen to me?" If that's your case, you have an advantage over even someone like me whose personal and professional life bears little resemblance to a significant portion of the social media audience I speak to, who, like you, are just getting started. That audience can relate better to the struggles and triumphs of someone trying to figure out how to flip their first house than the guy flipping hundreds of houses with the help of his full-time staff.

My couch-flipping videos offer a perfect example of this. As I described before, this was certainly not something I took up when I had it all figured out. In fact, it took months of trial and error before I even made it into something successful enough to pay the bills as initially intended. But I learned a ton through that journey, mainly through course-correcting from my missteps along the way.

Making those videos was like a reeducation from the lessons I learned through all that craziness. You really can't make a coherent video without reflecting on what you learned and what you have to offer. I know I've gained new insights just by looking back and documenting the good, the bad, and the ugly of that journey.

My couch-flipping videos remain some of my most popular, and I think that is because they are relatable. Let's face it, finding success in couch flipping feels more accessible to most people than real estate investing or starting a business. Besides, those who are contemplating a leap of faith into something more ambitious like house flipping can relate better to a person who is willing to openly broadcast the good and bad of their own experience taking that leap than someone who has been there, done that, and long since forgotten how bumpy the road was when they first started.

The point is that documenting your journey through online content creation represents a potential win-win. You benefit from the reflection involved in traditional journaling while providing guidance and inspiration to those who come across the content you create.

Action Items

Tim Ferriss describes journaling as "the most cost-effective therapy I've ever found."[27] Below are some ways to save on a shrink by putting it in ink:

1. **Regulate your use of social media.** As with so many other areas I discuss, your use of social media comes down to setting and adhering to your intentions. There are numerous ways to do this. Some apps like Facebook and Instagram offer menu options to track your activity, or you can download an app like RescueTime to track your time across platforms. If tracking is not enough, iPhone users can set a time limit for specific apps within phone settings. Whatever method you choose, the point is that you decide what amount of time and what type of content is acceptable and won't serve as a hindrance to your well-being.

2. **Aim for consistency, not quantity.** There's no need to write a certain number of pages or for a certain amount of time, but it is important to make journaling a habit. Not only will consistency make the practice easier, but it will also cultivate the accountability of being honest about how things are going in your internal and external world and what you need to keep doing or the changes that need to be made.

---

27 Tim Ferris, "What my morning journal looks like," Tim.Blog (blog), 15 January, 2015, https://tim.blog/2015/01/15/morning-pages/comment-page-7/.

3. **Practice "Thinking Time" from *The Road Less Stupid*.** [28] In the book, author Keith Cunningham suggests a method of journaling in which you take thirty to forty-five uninterrupted minutes twice a week to write down answers to difficult questions that force you to clarify your position on whatever issues you may be facing. *The Road Less Stupid* is one of my favorite books, and "Thinking Time," which I practice once a month has been an invaluable tool for coming up with solutions to persistent problems and clarifying my direction on new projects.

The Seeds of a Movement

Until 2020, I didn't have the time or the interest to keep up with social media. Or, more precisely, I didn't have the interest to make the time for social media. As you've seen, I am pretty selective about what I let onto my schedule, and at the time, I just didn't see the value in making content. But like everyone else, the pandemic turned my routine upside down. One day, I'm firing on all cylinders in real estate, on pace to flip about one hundred houses within the year, and the next, I'm locked down in my house, twiddling my thumbs and stewing in my thoughts.

But as you may have picked up by now, I'm not one to stew for very long before I start to zero in on some problem, which usually gives way to a project in no time. So as the days passed and society remained on pause, I began to look around and wonder what all this societal upheaval might mean for the direction the world was headed. And as I sat confined to my home along with everyone else, I found myself watching the YouTube channels of people like Graham Stephan and Kevin Paffrath of "Meet Kevin," guys who were freely sharing not just their expertise but also the millions of dollars they

---

28 Keith Cunningham, *The Road Less Stupid* (Austin: Keys to the Vault, 2017).

were bringing in through social media. There was no denying it: these guys weren't investing in real estate at the level I was, but they were investing in the social media game—and they were *killing* it.

Suddenly I realized something. If I, of all people, am sitting here watching these videos, then there's no telling how many others are spending their time doing the same thing. Granted, the popularity of social media was well-established by the time COVID-19 locked everything and everyone down, but I felt that the iron was hotter than it would ever be while everybody was stuck at home. But what did this have to do with me? Taking any interest in social media represented a fundamental perspective shift and challenged my own status quo. It was almost sport among my Mastermind buddies to hate on social media, and I frankly never thought of questioning that perspective.

So, in this state of cognitive dissonance, I sought solitude. I moved away from the noise and the distractions and into my conscience, looking to find out where I *really* stood relative to social media and how it fit with my values, my strengths and weaknesses, and my vision and my goals. As you can see from the journal entries that follow, I brainstormed and used "Thinking Time" to answer the questions that would establish my eventual strategy:

4-11-2020

- How do I become the most well-known real estate investor in the world?
- YouTube will play a major role.
- I need the "how-to" videos.
- I need a full-time videographer.
- I need a social media manager who knows how and when to post.
- I need to reach out to other influencers.

- I need to figure out the studio I want.

- I need content ideas.

4-18-2020

- Who do I want to cater my YouTube channel to?

- Beginners. I can build a program for beginners that is scalable.

- How-to videos, real-life negotiations, talks with my team, new office, more flash, more checks. I gotta go all in to see results.

- Should I edit my own videos?

5-3-2020

- What are viral video ideas?

- How I turned 10K into millions

- How I paid above-market value and made 100K

- Apartment complex with no payments

- How to find your first deal

- What are current YouTube trends?

- Stimulus

- Covid

- PPP loans

- EIDL loans

These ideas represent the fruits of my time alone in the morning, where I put everything I could think of onto a page to consider my potential place in the world of social media. Through this process,

I realized I had much to say and share and the perfect means to do so generously.

With all of this considered, I got going on the work necessary to take the risk (a calculated one) I was about to take. I got to work on educating myself, reading books, taking classes and courses, and learning from anything else I could get my hands on. Once I felt ready to take a calculated risk, my calculations told me that YouTube was the hottest iron in the fire. Since they were owned by Google, I knew that anything I put there would take precedence in web searches based solely on that. I reasoned, too, that those interested in real estate investing would prefer long-form content, even though I later discovered that they'd take to the bite-sized snacks of TikTok just as readily as they would the full course meals I prepared on YouTube.

Mostly, I made sure that my plan and eventual presence on YouTube and social media would offer a true reflection of who I was as a man in business and life and serve as an abundant source of information to those who it might reach. And as it turned out, it reached a lot. What started in solitude arrived at journaling in public and sharing my journey in the company of millions.

CHAPTER 8

Know Yourself

"If you want to do a few small things right, do them yourself. If you want to do great things and make a big impact, learn to delegate."

—JOHN MAXWELL

"What's taking them so long? They picked up that paint a week ago, and we still gotta install the flooring. Yeah, yeah, that tile can't stay, it's hideous."

Once I had finally acknowledged that my busyness had progressed to unmanageability, I turned to my dad for help managing all the projects I was trying to juggle on my own. I talked louder so he could hear me over the loud music, video games, and crude jokes coming from all directions in the clubhouse.

"Hold on, um, lemme call you back." With thirty minutes left until we had to take the field for warm-ups, an urgent email had arrived in my inbox. Meanwhile, I was the last guy still in his street clothes. But dang it, this couldn't wait!

"Hi, Sam. I am genuinely sorry for the oversight on the paper-work. I will fix the error by 9:00 a.m. tomorrow. I hope this does not jeopardize our working relationship."

"Pineda, get your crap on, we gotta be out there in fifteen minutes!"

It was time to hit the field, and I had forgotten to tell my dad the one thing I called to tell him.

The Cost of DIY

2017 was the first year in my life that I didn't enjoy baseball. Every game, I tried to cram in everything I could before I hit the field. And every time, I'd miss something, screw up something. The results were no different on the baseball diamond. Though I was there physically, I wasn't all there mentally, which showed in my performance: uncharacteristic blunders in the field, a batting average lower than I'd ever had in my career, and a general drop off in the competitive fire that had gotten me there in the first place. I played the game preoccupied with everything I didn't get to, eager for the game to end so I could rush back to the clubhouse and return all the calls and emails I'd missed while on the field. I was working my tail off, yet, I was underperforming professionally and athletically.

This period of flipping houses while still playing baseball taught me some hard-earned lessons on the perils of self-reliance. By now, you know the story. I found success at the end of the rabbit trail that started with an infomercial in a New Orleans hotel room and led to emptying my bank accounts and maxing out every credit card I could fit into my Mindy's and my wallets. Yet despite these early wins, I soon discovered that I was short on the other crucial resources that I would need to invest to continue my success in real estate investing: time and energy.

From sunup to sundown, from my living room to the clubhouse, I was grinding, doing everything I could to thrive in this new game of real estate investing while hanging onto the dream of a career in the game of baseball by a thread that was unraveling quickly. But by the time I slipped out of my baseball uniform and into work clothes, I was running on fumes. I was going from Superman to Clark Kent, not the other way around, and I needed to bring my best to be the best.

The End of My Rope

As the number of investments went up, so did the need to check on properties and the contractors' progress. Whatever scraps of time left over I spent looking for deals and driving back and forth endlessly, checking on properties and delivering checks whenever contractors came calling for their due.

I wasn't only responsible for overseeing the contractors' labor, but also for buying the materials they needed to do the job. The result was a codependent relationship with The Home Depot that began to seriously compromise my values. Like a needy partner, they were calling at all hours whenever one of my contractors showed up ready to buy materials. They needed my credit card information *right then*, and I would drop everything, no matter how important, to ensure that I was there at their whim. If I wasn't there, the materials wouldn't get bought, and the work wouldn't get done. It was as simple as that.

I reached my wit's end when I realized that this dysfunctional relationship was taking precedence over my relationship with God. It wasn't unusual for The Home Depot to call when I was in the middle of praying, and in my mind, I *had* to answer. *Sorry, God, but I have to let you go. The Home Depot is calling.*

Clearly, my business was expanding more quickly than my capacity to keep up. A year prior, I had contributed my hard-earned money toward the acquisition and flipping of twenty homes, fifteen more than during my first year flipping houses. A year after that, business only continued to grow, and I was on pace to more than double my properties. With a couple of years of experience under my belt and still playing professional baseball, my house flipping venture consisted of a Realtor, a lender, a project manager, and an acquisitions manager. Unfortunately, every one of those people was me.

I had taken on those roles by necessity, despite having neither the passion nor the expertise to execute them with the excellence I expected. I had a willingness to take risks. I had discipline. I had the humility to learn and grow from my mistakes. But already burned out *and* on the verge of six more months on the road playing baseball, I could see that these attributes had taken me as far as I could go; rapid growth had finally given way to diminishing returns.

I could also see with painful, exhausting clarity that it was time to find some help, more than my dad alone could provide in his spare time. Not only was *I* not enough, but I'd reached the point where the two contractors who had handled all of the rehabs up to that point were no longer cutting it either, and the last thing I wanted to do was deal with more contractors and more calls from my mistress, The Home Depot. I had more than twenty properties, each with a long checklist of tasks associated with my most dreaded aspect of the job: project management. Ensuring the jobs were done correctly and efficiently required crunching numbers, planning designs and repairs, and oversight of the two contractors, which would soon expand to several more.

I needed a person like me and, ideally, one who could thrive in the aspects of the job I hated the most that were about to get much more difficult. Luckily, I knew a person who I felt would make the perfect project manager, a person with unwavering character and a tireless work ethic—and also someone who knew next to nothing about the construction business. Crazy as it sounds, I didn't care about finding someone with an impressive resume or a ton of experience. What mattered to me was finding someone ready to learn and who I could trust without reservation. My friend Nick was the perfect man for the job.

The Wisdom of Overwhelm

There is nothing inherently wrong with feeling overwhelmed. In fact, sometimes it's a good thing. It might mean that business is booming. It's just booming too much for you to keep up. Feeling overwhelmed is a sign that your *busyness* can't keep up with your business.

You need to pay attention to what your feelings are telling you. What is the point of making tons of money if you're miserable? Whether you're short on money or short on time and energy, the result is the same: you feel overwhelmed.

When I started flipping houses, operating as a real estate agent for my own flips, finding deals wasn't just the fun part. It also drove my earning potential in a small fraction of my time. The rest of the time, I was spinning my wheels doing all the crap I had to do to seal the deals: writing listings, dealing with agents, writing contracts, and managing escrow. All that time spent entangled in the red tape was pulling me from what I was actually good at, what set me apart, excited me, and moved the needle.

It wasn't until I stepped back from my overwhelm and used my brain that I considered what it might actually mean to pull in some help. I was so focused on what I *could* do on my own that I hadn't seriously considered whether it was what I *should* be doing.

Nickel-and-diming dies hard. It's easy to fall into the I-can-do-this-myself-for-free trap. Yeah, you can do it for free, but it's important to ask yourself what value you're putting on the time you spend doing it.

The Importance of Knowing Yourself

Your strengths supply the 20 percent that will produce 80 percent of your results. That's why it is absolutely critical to be honest with yourself about your strengths and weaknesses and use that self-knowledge to leverage your time by exercising your strengths. Doing things any other way robs you of the hours of your life and the money in your pocket.

Some people hyperfocus on their weaknesses or try to overcome them by force of will. They ignore their nature, straining against the wind to complete tasks that could be delegated to another positioned to work with the wind at their back. In the process, they miss entirely how far they could get if all that time were freed to sharpen and wield the best weapons they were endowed with at birth. A phrase in military combat and sports applies here: "The best defense is a good offense."

The fact is, leaning into your weaknesses *should* feel unnatural. It should serve as a signal that you are doing something that's not intended for you. There is a quote often attributed to Albert Einstein that says, "Everyone is a genius. But if you judge a fish by its ability to climb a tree, it will live its wholelife believing that it is stupid."[29] When I started as a real estate agent, I felt like Einstein on the baseball field and the fourth Stooge when I stepped off the field. There was a reason (maybe a few reasons) that I wasn't successful as a real estate agent. Busy work, creating listings, writing contracts, and all the other detail-oriented tasks make me want to run out into traffic.

And guess what? The fact that others loved to do those things represented a golden opportunity for reciprocity in action. Your inconvenience is another person's indulgence. Delegating the tasks you hate may offer someone else the chance to earn a living by exercising their gifts.

---

29 Nayeli Lomeli, "Fact Check: No, Albert Einstein Did Not Say Famous Quote About Fish Climbing Trees," *USA Today,* April 27, 2021, "https://www.usatoday.com/story/news/fact-check/2021/04/27/fact-check-einstein-never-said-quote-fish-climbing-trees/7384370002/

Delegate to Elevate

In business, there's a saying, delegate to elevate. No matter who you are, no matter how productive or multi-talented, there is a ceiling of growth for you and your business when you try to do it all on your own.

Letting pride get in the way of delegating and hiring is easy. Some people rationalize that they won't share their tasks because another person won't do them as well as you do. That could be true, but you alone can only do so much. Let's say you're working for eight hours at 100 percent efficiency, and two others are working at 80 percent. Yes, you may have worked more consistently, but you were still outworked. You completed a total of eight hours of work in the same time that they did almost thirteen. In the meantime, you lost eight extra hours when you could have been doing something else. Hiring is buying time; I buy their time, and they free up mine.

When I finally stopped being so stubborn about doing everything myself, I discovered how much I'd been harming my emotional *and* financial well-being. As it turned out, the cost of a project manager and a real estate agent was a few thousand dollars, chump change when each deal netted somewhere in the ballpark of twenty to thirty thousand dollars, not to mention all of the other deals done with the time left over that paid for my hires ten times over.

It was among the most significant reliefs of my life, not to mention one of the biggest epiphanies. I realized that I would be an idiot to waste time and money trying to juggle everything myself, making chump change when I could be doing what I did best: making the kind of deals that brought in tens of thousands of dollars, even up to six and seven figures. I liked making deals. After all, deals make money.

By delegating the work, I got back my most valuable resource for doing just that—my time. Delegation and hiring grow your business by freeing up time to focus on those skills that produce 80 percent of your results and make space for a life beyond your work. The result is financial growth and, even more important, the time to invest those profits into your well-being. Doing every task yourself is not efficient. It's impossible to do it all and adhere to Pareto's Principle, focusing on high-level, high-impact professional or personal activities.

Granted, the amount that you delegate will depend greatly on life circumstances. If you're an employee, your job is essentially being delegated to accomplish the company's overarching mission. Still, take a step back, and you may find that some aspects of life are better done by someone else.

Let's take mowing the lawn as an example. The going rate for that job would be about twenty dollars an hour, give or take a few dollars. So the question is: How much is your time worth? Essentially, you are committing an hour of your time to this task and, by doing so, agreeing that you are willing to work for twenty dollars an hour. Is there something you could be doing with that hour worth more than that? Is there something you could be doing to build your business? Perhaps you could invest that time in your family or your health. How much is your time worth? That's for you to decide.

Action Items

Abundance in all areas of life starts with knowledge of self. Without a solid understanding of your strengths and liabilities, you're destined to become overwhelmed when you've reached progress's ceiling and your busyness has outpaced your business. You must have the humility to ask for help. The suggestions below will help you better determine when it's time to let others shoulder your burdens:

1. **Identify your strengths through a personality test.** Depending on the one you use, a personality test can offer a shortcut to determining your signature strengths and the areas in which you are likely to thrive. I invest a good deal of money on the one I administer to students and prospective employees called

the Predictive Index, but there are many free options online, including the Signature Strengths Questionnaire (https://strengthsbasedresilience.com/assessment) and Tony Robbins's DISC Assessment (https://www.tonyrobbins.com/disc/).

2. **Know your worth.** Figure out how much your employer thinks you're worth. Let's say you're making a hundred thousand dollars. If you're working forty hours a week for fifty weeks, assuming you take a couple weeks off for vacation, then you're working two thousand hours a year. Divide your salary by the total hours worked, and you'll find that your employer thinks you're worth fifty dollars an hour. Do you believe you're worth less or more?

3. **Read *Traction* by Gino Wickman.** This book has drastically grown my business with its lessons on hiring and delegating tasks that don't align with one's strengths and interests.[30]

Better Together

With Nick on board, business took off. Nick was managing all the projects and overseeing all the contractors, freeing up my time to focus on finding great deals. The result was fifty homes by the end of the year, up from twenty the year prior. It wasn't long after that that Nick had worked himself out of the job, handing off his project management duties to a new hire and leveraging his talents as a broker. Our collaboration then gave way to a new brokerage business and more opportunities for the individuals we would recruit to help us continue to grow and leverage our strengths.

Though burnout and six months of unrelenting travel playing ball in the minors initially convinced me I needed to share the load

---

30 Gino Wickman, *Traction: Get a Grip on Your Business.* (New York : BenBella Books, Inc., 2012).

with someone else, I was wholly sold on delegation by the time I was released from the A's. Untethered by a demanding practice schedule and half of the year on the road, I suddenly found my time multiplied, my discipline primed, and my clarity sharpened. I knew what I needed to do to scale even further. I hired more project managers. I brought on board real estate agents, acquisitions managers, cold-callers, and even my sister, who now serves as the COO of my parent company.

Five years later, I now run seven businesses. I've flipped homes and apartment units by the hundreds. I produce social media content every day for over a million followers. And despite all of this, I spend more time with my family and on the things I love doing more than most people who make forty thousand dollars a year. Thanks to delegation, I only do the things I like to do and feel far less overwhelmed than I did when I was bringing in exponentially less income.

It's easy to get so adamant about your self-sufficiency that you miss this win-win scenario. The feeling of overwhelm is your friend. It's telling you to get out of the way of your own progress, and another's opportunity. It's telling you to go find some help.

CHAPTER 9

Track Your Wealth

"If you fail to plan, you are planning to fail."

—BENJAMIN FRANKLIN

"Good morning, everyone!"

You scan the auditorium, an ocean of faces united in admiration and giddy anticipation for the TED Talk they have come all of this way to see you deliver. Your voice, upbeat and welcoming, cuts through the thunderous applause that accompanies your breezy stroll to center stage. A chorus of voices echoes your greeting and tone: "Good morning!"

You are in your element, dressed to the nines, completely secure in your mastery of the material you are about to deliver, oozing with charisma and vigor so palpable that it's felt no less in the nosebleeds than the stage. "How is everyone today?" you ask, to which the crowd offers a raucous response not typical of such a generic opening. As the replies die out, a high-pitched yell comes from the back. "We love you!" Everyone laughs in approval.

Emboldened, you go off-script and dive right into a joke, the kind you deliver with anticipation that grows exponentially as you near the punchline, knowing howls of laughter will follow right on its heels. "Have you heard about the real estate investor who moonlights as a detective?"

Brrring!

The alarm jars you from the TED Talk of your dreams. You have to be at work in an hour, and you didn't even get to hear the punch-line,[31] much less the hoots and hollers of your throes of adoring fans. You slam your fist on the alarm clock to delay reality by ten minutes and hope you can return to your fantasy, but you lay there instead, finally beginning to drift in time for the alarm to demand again that you get up and face the music.

The What and The Why

This is the reality of many nine-to-fivers. Their goals don't change much from day-to-day. Arrive at work close enough to nine that no one will notice. Once there, do just enough work that, again, no one will notice. These goals, alongside all of the other duties assigned on a given day, work toward the one and only unspoken goal that means the most to that person: get home to check out for the evening and get to Friday to check out for two days.

This is a life driven by urgency and obligation, where the only goal that seems appealing is escaping those imposed by others—not exactly a recipe for empowerment and fulfillment. Granted, maybe they daydream about something more—when loading couches into storage units, I know I did. But the old adage is true: "A goal without a plan is just a dream."

The truth is, if you are not setting goals, you are shooting yourself in the foot. This is not my opinion; this is a fact. Research has

---

31 The silver lining is that the audience was spared the punchline...the real estate investor/ detective's name was "Sherlock Holmes".

demonstrated that people who set goals outperform those who don't.[32] Really, it's common sense. Let's take push-ups as an example. Will someone do thirty push-ups if they haven't set a goal? Probably not.

There are two invisible benefits to setting goals: motivation and self-efficacy. I'll cover the latter in the next section. As for motivation, it's not a good goal if the goal does not get you moving. There are a couple of reasons why this might be the case.

First, goals divorced from values won't contain the fuel from your heart's answer to "why?" For example, in chapter five, we discussed the futility of keeping up with the Joneses. If you're comparing yourself to others and trying to live up to *their* values, you're operating on a gas tank with a hole in the bottom. The long-range goals likely to hold your attention are built upon the things that matter to you. Your values provide the "why," and long-term goals answer the "what?"

So not only are goals that have nothing to do with your deeply held convictions likely to fail, but the ones that don't are destined to take you somewhere that doesn't bring about satisfaction anyway. So, a perfect recipe for a life of frustration is to ignore your values as you go about your life, choosing your next action and the next based on urgency until the urgent is eliminated and you can finally rest—or, more likely, just hide.

Get SMART

Some goals fail to produce motivation because they don't align with your values. Others because the vision related to the goal isn't clear. A vision is a necessary component of the goal-setting process. Let's go back to push-ups. If the reason behind those thirty push-ups is

---

32 Matthews, G. (2015). Goal Research Summary. Paper presented at the 9th Annual International Conference of the Psychology Research Unit of Athens Institute for Education and Research (ATINER), Athens, Greece.

that a stranger suddenly demands that you stop and give them thirty, then motivation will probably be low, and confusion will definitely be high. But if your vision of vibrant health and a healthy heart is behind the decision to pursue strength training (and push-ups are a specific action of that pursuit), then you will find a reason to push through the struggle.

But what if your goal doesn't go beyond improving your heart health? In that case, you are right back to daydreaming. Long-term goals provide the "what" but not the "how." Ultimately, the purpose of goals is direction. You must be your own coach, who sets the drills that lead to the desired outcome. You can set goals that don't give you any real, tangible direction and therefore don't do you any good. And that's where the "smart" in SMART goals come in.

A baseball coach doesn't say: "All right, start practicing," and then kicks back in the dugout for an hour. He says, "First, we're going to take fifteen minutes of grounders, then move on to a half hour of batting practice." He assigns the tasks that align with the intermediate goals of improving hitting and fielding, increasing the likelihood of fulfilling the vision of winning a championship, and he does so unambiguously, making clear the standards. This is the purpose of a SMART goal: Specific, Measurable, Attainable, Relevant, and Time-bound.

Fifteen minutes of grounders is a specific goal: It clearly states the required time and action. It is measurable. When the clock hits fifteen minutes, then the goal is completed. It's attainable, not so difficult or strenuous that it leads to discouragement, nor so easy that it becomes boring. It is relevant, assuming all players value sharpening their skills and winning a championship. Finally, it is time-bound and clear about when it is to occur and how long it must go on until it is complete. Of course, a player could set a similar goal himself, something along the lines of, "I will take thirty minutes of batting practice by Friday at five p.m." Again, the criteria is specific, the difficulty appropriate, and bound to a specific amount of time for its completion.

Again, there is extensive evidence that goals work, and there's further and undeniable evidence that SMART goals work best.[33] They work because they assign clear direction and therefore establish firm self-accountability. Without a clear agenda, you live at the mercy of your impulses and your place in life, now and in the future.

Returning one more time to push-ups, who will do thirty push-ups? Bob, who set the goal to do thirty push-ups at seven in the morning after his 6:30 a.m. alarm buzzes, pulls on the shorts and shirt he's laid out the night before, or Bill, who plans to do some push-ups sometime tomorrow? Who's more likely to feel discouraged and frustrated with his progress over time, wondering why he can't seem to get his act together? Well, Bob literally got his act together before he set out to perform it. On the other hand, Bill didn't bother determining the time or criteria that he deemed a job well done.

The purpose of goals is direction. They are the plans that breathe life into the vision. Goals keep your reactiveness and mindless busyness in check, setting you on the path you *want* to be on—not the place you find yourself because you couldn't focus.

A One-Stop Shop

I take my time seriously. As a Christian, I treat each moment on Earth as a gift and preparation for life in Heaven. I don't believe that my time ends when it all runs out here, but that doesn't mean I treat my days as though I have all the time in the world. I believe my life has a purpose, so I strive daily to take full advantage of the gifts I've

---

33 Hyrum Smith, *10 Natural Laws of Successful Time and Life Management* (New York: Warner Books, 1994).

been given to carry out that purpose. I treat every new day like a blank page where I write my life story, and each one counts.

For years, I've carried that perspective into my approach to each morning, intending to prepare my body, mind, and spirit to perform all the plans I make for that day to the best of my abilities. I've already described my morning routine to you: up at six, straight to the shower, read the Bible, spend some time in prayer, write in my journal, and then finally, I am ready to turn my attention to the topic of this chapter, the Wealthy Way Planner.

I established this routine just like anything else in my life, through trial and error. Though working with a planner always played a role in that routine, I could never find one that met all of my needs. Gratitude journals, bullet journals, run-of-the-mill day planners— you name it, I tried it. But still, all of them fell short of meeting my needs.

I needed a one-stop shop, a day planner, gratitude journal, prayer list, and an archive and tracker of my long-term, short-term, and daily goals, all rolled into one. Was that too much to ask? Well, once I'd accepted that the answer seemed to be yes, I decided to make my own. I created a system in Google Sheets that brought together all those needs and allowed me to fill out and track everything in one place. It was everything that I wanted in a journal. It was comprehensive. It was personalizable and interactive, and after a while, I decided it was too helpful to keep to myself. So I hired a couple developers and asked them if we could pretty it up and make it a bit less complex and more user-friendly. The result was the Wealthy Way Planner.

The Wealthy Way Planner

How would your life look in five years if you could have it any way you wanted? What are your family and social life like? How about your material things and belongings? What are you driving? Where are you living? What's the state of your career? How about your health?

The answers to these questions will be the foundation of your goals for the year, guiding your weekly goals, daily tasks, and moment-to-moment decisions. It's easy to get overwhelmed by the audacity of your vision, the gap between where you are today and where you'd like to be five years from now. The key is to not get bogged down by the journey and focus on the individual steps that will get you there. Even a relatively short-term goal, like losing five pounds, is absolutely useless without specific actions guiding each and every one of the thirty days that will get you there. The only way to achieve a distant vision is to focus on the process and leave the outcome to its own devices. Focusing on the outcome without defining the course accomplishes nothing but discouragement.

That's where the Wealthy Way Planner comes in, which you can access for free, no-strings-attached at wealthyway.com or by downloading the mobile app. The planner I created walks you through each step that culminates in a commitment to action, immediate, purpose-driven action that will keep you on track to an abundant future.

The first step in the process is to establish a vision. It's easy to get caught up in the day-to-day hustle and completely miss the fact that none of the things you are doing are moving you toward your desired life. That's why establishing a vision of your best life and ideal future comes before goals and the work required to get you there.

I created the WEALTH acronym to represent the six areas of wealth that comprise a vision of true prosperity: **W**orship, **E**ducation, **A**ffluence, **L**ifestyle, **T**eam, and **H**ealth. I believe living in these values will set you up to live an abundant life. I cover each extensively in part three, but for now, here is a brief description of each:

- **Worship** means how you feed your spirit and can refer to any spiritual act, prayer, meditation, serving, reading scripture, and donating/tithing.

- **Education** refers to time devoted to self-development, such as listening to podcasts, reading books, going to seminars, and hiring mentors and coaches.

- **Affluence** relates to your money and how you build financial wealth, whether through investing, your career, leveraging taxes to your benefit, or building businesses and companies.

- **Lifestyle** is about the fruits of your labor: your car, your house, vacations, and the budget that sustains it all.

- **Team** is your family and friends, employees and coworkers. Wealth in this area comes through any action aimed at making these relationships flourish.

- **Health** comprises your diet, workouts, and everything else that keeps you fit enough to achieve your goal.

Live fully in all these areas, and you will live in abundance. Focus on affluence at the expense of your family and friends, and you will be socially broke. Focus on lifestyle at the expense of affluence, and you will be financially broke. An abundant life requires that none of these areas be neglected daily. But choosing those actions starts with a vision.

I suggest starting with a five-year vision, broken down into the five aspects of WEALTH building. Unlike your SMART goals, these should be audacious. This is your opportunity to dream big, attainability aside, without reservation or filter. After all, five years is a long time from now. Maybe you live in a tiny apartment but dream of owning a million-dollar home in five years. Your role in this step is to claim it.

After you set your five-year vision, determine where you want to be one year from now. Set one to three goals for every letter of the WEALTH acronym for the following year. The key here is to set specific goals so it's clear at the end of the year: you either reached them or you didn't. Let's say, for example, you set a Lifestyle goal to buy a Tesla within a year. Whether or not you reach this goal is black or white; you're either charging up your new Tesla by day 365, or you're still pumping gas into your Corolla. The same goes for a goal assigned a number value. If your goal is to donate time or money, you wouldn't say, "In a year, I want to donate money." Instead, you would say, "I want to donate twelve thousand dollars to my church this year." Again, there's no wiggle room on the goal criteria.

Although these annual goals are subject to change, you should take the time to reflect on what really matters to you, ensuring that the goals you choose represent accomplishments that would truly bring you happiness and fulfillment. Not only that, but these goals will serve as the signpost to your daily priorities—how you use time, your most precious resource. Reflection ensures that these goals represent what's important enough to you to keep you pushing when things are tough.

You'll see all this on the dashboard, where you'll spend most of your time using the Wealthy Way Planner. It's where the rubber meets the road each day, continually driving you toward fulfilling your aspirations a year from now. Here, you will declare your three most important goals for the week, affirming your vision and reminding you of your priorities and desires.

Each morning, you will review your commitments and simply record whether you kept them. This is accountability, the kind that simply won't happen if you start the day reactively or reflexively, jumping right into your habitual way of doing things without considering whether they are effective or moving you to a future you'll like when you get there.

After you've reviewed and reaffirmed your accountability to your daily and yearly goals, it's time to take stock of the things that you are grateful for: the health of your loved ones, the roof over your head, or maybe even the mistakes that you made and the lessons you learned as a result. As insignificant as it may seem, this can completely shift your mindset and make you more cognizant of your life's blessings that may otherwise be taken for granted.

The same can be said for the final component and the topic of the last chapter, journaling. Again, there is no right or wrong way to journal. Journaling is about getting honest with yourself and giving expression to whatever is on your mind and heart. This can be just a random outflow of thoughts. It can be positive affirmations, reflections on the previous day, what went wrong, and how it can be corrected. It can be prayers, perhaps the aspect I've found most enriching. And that's the point. Not some particular agenda or format. It's about being open and honest, experimenting without reservations, and fig-uring out what works best for you.

All the while, you are monitoring and updating the progress on your weekly goals, recording when you've completed them. As you do so, the progress toward your yearly goals will be updated on the dashboard. Did you donate one of the twelve thousand dollars you committed? That will show up on your yearly total. And across the top, you will find perhaps the most powerful tool, the ticker remind-ing you of what you decided mattered to you, what you committed to going after—the person you want to be. These consistent reminders are the anchor that keeps you from drifting off course to things that don't matter to you and places you wouldn't have chosen to be. This has led to most of the success I have had in life. Reminders of what I want and why I'm doing what I'm doing.

The Wealthy Way Planner is my accountability partner. It doesn't lie about what I've declared that I want and how I'm progressing in those areas. Every morning, I am reminded of my goals, how much distance I've covered, and how far I have to go. I'm reminded that I have much to be grateful for. And through journaling, I have a heart-to-heart, man-to-man with myself to find out how I feel about where I'm at and where I'm headed. So when I step away, I am grounded, and I am focused. I am ready to take on the day.

Action Items

True abundance that spans all areas of life begins with mapping where you are relative to where you dream of being and coupling that understanding with specific goals and actions relevant to your overarching vision. The following are some ways you can get started on the path to WEALTH:

1. **Sign up for the Wealthy Way Planner at WealthyWay.com.** It's free and will walk you step-by-step through the process of turning your vision into the goals and actions that lead to true wealth.

2. **Establish a SMART goal for holding yourself accountable to using the Wealthy Way Planner.** Committing fifteen to thirty minutes to this first thing in the morning will allow you to plan your day around where you stand relative to your yearly and weekly goals—before you get caught up in the busyness of the day.

3. **Make a goal you are currently pursuing SMART.** Let's say you are trying to establish the habit of reading more. Make sure you state your intention so it is specific, measurable, attainable, relevant, and time-bound. Instead of writing: *Read more,* try something like, *I will read for three hours a week by reading in bed every Monday to Saturday from 9:30 p.m.-10:00 p.m."*

A SMART Husband

It would be easy for me to take for granted how blessed I am to have Mindy as my wife among all the commotion and busyness of life. She is my biggest supporter and cheerleader and a constant source of encouragement, inspiration, and grace in my life. One morning, reflecting on how fortunate I was and determined to show her how special she was to me, I wrote the following in my journal:

8-29-21

- What can I do to be a better husband to Mindy?
- Cook for her
- Tell her I love her every day
- Greet her with attention and affection
- Offer her more verbal praise and appreciation
- Send her occasional texts throughout the day
- Be more spontaneous and surprise her more often
- Buy her gifts, send her flowers
- Tell her she's beautiful
- Overall, be more intentional

From there, I set the intention to tell my wife I loved her every day. I chose this as a single behavior that would represent the type of husband I wanted to be—one who does not take his wife for granted and does not neglect to verbalize his love and appreciation consistently. I made it SMART to ensure that I was clear on my commitment. I wrote it down in my Wealthy Way Planner, which I treat like a contract of commitment to myself, one I know I will have to answer every day when I record whether I met the terms of that commitment.

Sure, something like saying *I love you* might seem unnecessary and unimportant to me some days, just as it might for her to hear it. But there's a saying, "Small choices become actions, actions become habits, and habits become our way of life." Over time, failing to remind Mindy that I love her would also become a habit, and the occasional *I love you* the exception. Over time, that would add up to the husband I am, whether that be one who appreciates his wife or one who takes her for granted. Though small, it's the type of habit that will eventually lead to a stronger or weaker relationship with my wife.

It all comes down to investment. The values that I affirm through my habits eventually become my character. So I, for one, choose not to leave that to chance. I sign up, follow through, and check back over and over again until, eventually, I'm a changed man.

Are you living the Wealthy Way?

One of the keys to living the Wealthy Way is being more self aware of your strengths and weaknesses. I've created a quiz to help you figure out what those are!

Take a couple of minutes to follow the link below and complete the Wealthy Way quiz. With your responses, we'll generate a personalized profile identifying the areas where you are flourishing and the areas that are holding you back from living a life of true abundance.

Once you've completed the quiz, *we'll email you access to my Wealth Builder Academy ($995 value)* to teach you the ins and outs of living the Wealthy Way and links to download our Wealthy Way mobile app and join our private Facebook group.

↓

WEALTHYWAY.COM/QUIZ-INTRO

PART III

Wealth

CHAPTER 10

Give Your Life to Something Greater Than Yourself

*"There's One Person above all others who desires an
extraordinary life for you. He is a Father who delights, like
any good father, in the achievements and happiness of His
children. His name is God! And nothing will please Him
more than seeing you reach your highest potential."*

—JOHN BEVERE

Becoming a wealth builder and living a life of true abundance comes down to intentionality and commitment. It does not happen by accident. It does not happen without effort. It is a matter of using your time wisely—choosing actions that lead to growth in each area that produces well-being far beyond the financial.

But just as financial abundance grows from the investments you make into your skills and your assets, so does abundance in all other areas of your life. It comes down to growing your wealth in each area of life through applying the aspects of the wealth builder mindset covered in part one: willingness to take risks for the sake of growth, exercising discipline, embodying a spirit of generosity, and humbly committing to your own path and purpose. These are the ways of being that ensure we are consistently responsible in caring for the gifts entrusted to us: our mind, body, spirit, our family, friends, coworkers, and, yes, also our money and belongings.

Now, I know not everyone reading this book is Christian. For those who are not, I want you to understand my intention isn't to offend or alienate you—far from it. I am here to inform you of what I know and share what has worked for me in hopes that it will lead to wealth and abundance in your life. I am not here to judge, impose my views onto you, or tell you yours are wrong. But it would be disingenuous for me to offer you my advice for abundant living and leave out what I consider the wellspring of my own abundance, which is my relationship with God.

Worship

The first aspect of WEALTH and the one that takes the highest priority in *my* life is worship. As a Christian, I constantly pursue a more intimate relationship with Jesus, who I believe to be the son of God. As I already shared, I believe that "the end" is actually "to be continued." As such, I view this world and all of the bells and whistles that keep us distracted from the spiritual side of life to be temporary and pale compared to the whole story.

So, regardless of the topic, whether that be goals, discipline, time management, or anything else, my mentality ultimately comes down to taking advantage of the opportunity to live, to use my life wisely and graciously for the glorification of Jesus through the betterment of the world and my fellow man. For me, it is about doing all that I can today to prepare for what comes next. Many would prefer not to ponder the end or what comes next, but what is more critical? It ends the same for all of us, so in my view, it would be negligent not to try and take full advantage of the days we are allotted in preparation for when they inevitably expire.

Again, I am not here to preach to you or convert you. I prefer to let my character speak louder than my words. But it would be inauthentic to leave out the place that faith holds in my life and remiss to deprive you of the tools that I view as foundational to my personal and professional successes. What I offer are some tried and true tools of the Spirit, tools that grow you from the inside out and bring peace and clarity of purpose to your movement and growth through all areas of your life.

I don't believe that true success exists without purpose. In my view, a lack of purpose leaves a spiritual void that cannot be filled with things external and material: more excitement, more entertainment, more money, and more busyness. None of those things result in more depth. Sure, they may provide a temporary distraction or a boost to the ego, but they are ultimately no more than ploys that allow a person to ignore what would be there if all those distractions and facades were taken away.

So, I begin each day intending to fill and prepare my spirit to live and serve with integrity, and I know from experience the difference it makes when I fail to do so. When I start my day by reading the Bible and praying, I and those around me will be better off. These practices directly affect the attitude I bring to the day and how I relate to myself and those I come in contact with. I start my day in worship because I have learned that I do myself a disservice starting it in any other way.

Prayer

You'd be hard pressed to find a religious tradition, Christian or otherwise, where prayer is not encouraged as a path to spiritual growth.

But it is prescribed far less often than explained, and the act of prayer is as multifaceted as the personalities and the reasons people pray.

Whatever its form, prayer comes down to talking to God however you see fit. It comes down to expressing yourself without reservation to Him, offering your complaints, frustrations, praises, and celebrations. If you are a believer, you probably believe that you can't hide from God, so prayer is as much about being honest with yourself before God as it is about being honest with Him.

Maybe the most important thing to remember when it comes to prayer is that, just as it goes with any person in your life, the depth and quality of your relationship to God depends on how consistently you offer your time and presence. You don't forge a good, trusting relationship with anyone if you never call. You'll never come to understand another's perspective if you don't spend any time with them. On the other hand, you can just about predict the next words out of the mouth of the person you spend every day with. It's far less about what you say than just showing up daily. There is no "right" way to pray. What's important is to show up and open up to yourself and God.

It is typical for me to commit about ten minutes to converse with God every morning. I'm not dogmatic about the practice; I don't set a timer to make sure I talk for ten minutes or stop mid-sentence and check "pray" off the to-do list once I've met that quota. What is important to me is to set enough time aside to truly disconnect from distraction, connect with God, and ensure that I stay honest with myself and Jesus. Some would call that too much, and some would claim it is not enough, but those opinions are not my concern or my business. Ten minutes represents the time I can remain fully present and finish feeling nourished in my spirit. Sometimes, I might need more, sometimes less. But that time may be different for you, and as with anything else, it is okay to start small and build up. Spiritual health is no different from physical health in that way. You will be able to handle more and get more from it the longer and more consistently you show up.

This is my philosophy on prayer: in Jesus, I have a direct relationship with the one who created me and the boundless universe that I am a part of. There is never a time when this belief is lost in how I pray. I offer love, gratitude, and praise for the gift of my existence, the sense of comfort and meaning that His presence brings to all I do, and the many blessings he's laid along my path.

Naturally, I also turn to Jesus when seeking purpose and direction in the life He created. When you want to learn how to use a new gadget, you open the instruction booklet provided by its creator. In the same way, when I need guidance on right living, I don't turn to YouTube or Google. I don't ask my mom or my friend. I turn directly to my Creator.

So, whenever I've felt lost, and the times have been many, the first thing I do is turn to God. Of course, I am going to turn to him in trying to navigate through troubles and uncertainties. Of course, I don't possess the wisdom to navigate my way through life's endless complexities and make all the right decisions. I *know* I don't have the answers, but I know the One who does. And so, I humble myself and seek His direction. I say, "God, I need help," and then I wait expectantly for him to direct me.

In fact, through prayer I ultimately decided to include worship in this chapter, knowing that it would turn some off. My conscience told me to let go of my fears and doubts about backlash, alienating and losing followers or business, and be true to the place of Jesus in my life and my heart.

Meditation

If prayer represents conversing with God, then meditation offers the alternative of sitting quietly and receptively with God or, if you are not a believer, your conscience. In meditation, you step away from the noise to center yourself; to seek internal quiet among the external noise.

Through meditation, you tune in and cultivate calm and stillness within yourself and your spirit.

You can expect that this may be difficult. Despite popular depictions of the blissful, Zenned-out monk, it's not meant to be easy. Is getting buff supposed to be easy? No! Neither is getting quiet. No matter how long a person meditates, they will still contend with their busy mind. The only difference is that the person who has tuned in most frequently has learned to bear the weight of their thoughts more gracefully.

So, if you have never meditated, expect to be uncomfortable initially. Apps like Calm can guide you through the process because it can feel very unnatural to sit in quiet and stillness, especially in today's world of bluster and information overload. So expect to be jerked around by the internal noise you typically drown out through busyness and other everyday distractions. But also know that if you keep showing up, you will eventually cultivate a quiet that persists amid the internal and external noise.

Scripture Reading

Many will devour every self-help book they can get their hands on but scoff at one of the oldest, most imitated, and most influential books of wisdom ever written. This book has stood the test of time, and one would be hard pressed to find one on self-improvement and good living that does not echo some of the sentiments and principles contained within its pages. Regardless of who you are and what you believe, the Bible is chock-full of stories and guidance that can drastically improve your life and make you a better and happier human being.

Most people don't realize how many common phrases come straight from the pages of the Bible. Have you been "fighting the good fight" but now find yourself "at your wit's end?" You keep plugging away because you know that "it's better to give than receive." You keep "going the extra mile" because you will eventually "reap what you sow." The problem is, the money you're making is "a drop in the bucket" compared to what you could be making, but you know deep down that "the love of money is the root of all evil." Besides, this is your true "labor of love," and it beats working for "the powers that be" any day of the week. The truth is, it's "a double-edged sword" either way you cut it. Yes, sometimes what you're trying to accomplish for others can feel like "the blind leading the blind." But even on the days that you "escape by the skin of your teeth," you'll "rise and shine" again the next day, knowing that you're following your conscience. And sometimes, you just have to "eat, drink, and be merry."

Yep, every single one of those phrases comes from the Bible.

Many of the principles you live by daily may come from the Bible and you don't even realize it. And here's a secret: many of the principles in this book come from the Bible, and the reason is that one, I'm a Christian and, two, they work no matter what you believe. So, when I'm asked what self-help books I read, there's just one answer, and the reason for that is that it covers *everything*. I never encounter a scenario in my business or personal life that the Bible can't help me address. By all means, read self-help books. But I stick to the Bible because I find that "there's nothing new under the sun" (Ecclesiastes 1:9).

You may not believe everything you read there. That's fine. But you would be hard pressed to give the Bible an earnest reading and not come away without some food for thought, bits and pieces that improve the way you view the world and your place in it.

Service

It's human nature to act first with an eye toward how your actions benefit yourself, and I am no exception. As you have probably gathered, I am obsessed with using my time wisely, and often what I see as wise comes down to one question: Am I going to make the most profit doing this? Well, have you heard the phrase, "It's better to give than receive?" How about, "The love of money is the root of all evil?" Those come from the Bible, and they're in there because we all need reminders.

It's a weird paradox that what benefits us most is often what we can do to help our fellow man. Our selfish appetites never seem satiated, but service is the answer. You'll find that more money, more stuff, and more fun is never enough. If your only objective is accumulating more for yourself, you are destined to be dissatisfied. The best rewards, the ones that bring fulfillment and cannot be taken away, are those you earn through service.

From a surface financial perspective, volunteering seems like a terrible use of time. Indeed, what you reap from sowing with generosity may not be financial gain. But what you do gain internally lasts beyond financial gain. Volunteering opens your mind and expands your perspective. It fosters gratitude for what you have and also reveals the value you have to offer to those in need.

I learned this most deeply through my time volunteering with the charity Homes for Hope and building homes for impoverished families in Mexico. It took two to three days of our time to build a house from the bottom-up, an insignificant amount of time in the grand scheme of our lives. Yet, those few days of our lives potentially changed the rest of theirs.

Witnessing the joy of that family as they gazed upon the home that some would view as a shack in America left me with a sense of fulfillment that remains with me today. Not only that, but seeing the depths of that family's gratitude gave me a new perspective of how immensely fortunate I am to take such blessings for granted. Six kids, no running water, inadequate food, yet they were running around, shoeless, smiling, happy just to be alive. Meanwhile, I was discontent about the size of my house, the taste of my food, and people's perception of me on social media.

I hope you will seek out the unrivaled opportunity to help yourself by helping others. In my view, there is no greater generosity than that of your most valuable resources—your time and energy. You don't get time back. You don't get energy back. What more charitable gifts can a person offer than the ones that can't be repaid but simultaneously make the time you have left that much richer?

Donating

What topic would you guess comes up most in the Bible? Is it heaven and hell? Is it prayer? Faith, maybe? Nope, the number one topic is money because money represents our greatest temptation toward selfishness. Money can fool us into thinking we don't need our brothers and sisters and they don't need us. We'll just take all of the riches around us for ourselves, claiming that what's mine is mine, and yours is yours.

Luke 16:10 pretty much sums it up: "Whoever can be trusted with very little can also be trusted with much, and whoever is dishonest with very little will also be dishonest with much." Money managed correctly should make you better as a person, not worse. Money should be a tool to affirm and further the reach of your values.

In the last section, I wrote that I see time and money as the most generous gifts we can offer. Of course, that's a matter of perception. Some see money as their greatest resource and thus the greatest sacrifice they can offer another. They see time as the slave to money, not the other way around. Whether or not that be the case, donating provides an antidote to the trappings of greed, that tight-fisted perspective that never allows a person to be satisfied with the size of their bank account.

The way you view your money is a reflection of what you feel inside. If you want all the money to yourself, that speaks volumes about spirit and your views of community and connectedness to your fellow man and woman. But consider this: What good is money if it only tightens your grip, if it feeds your preoccupation with losing it instead granting you the freedom to use it for good? What good is money that's hoarded for your own gain? What's the point of the false sense of superiority that keeps you separate instead of bringing you closer to others? What's the point of money if not to lift up those around you?

Of course, many of you reading this who are not so fortunate may say, "Well, this will have to wait until later." While I have been there, done that, and definitely understand those thoughts, I contend that financial generosity does not depend on your income. One person's dollar is another's thousand dollars.

Those who can be trusted with little can be trusted with much because money only amplifies the person you are, whether you are generous or stingy. Whether or not your bank account reflects abundance as society defines it, that tight-fisted, loss-aversive, fear-based mentality will linger with every zero you may eventually add to your income.

I'll say it again: generosity is the antidote to greed and the pride that goes along with it. It is also the antidote to the internal sense of scarcity that manifests externally as stinginess and fear. Make it your goal and your pride to lift others up. Show your gratitude for your fortune by helping others who have not had the chips fall in their favor. Giving is a habit and a way of life. The spirit is the same, that of investing in the well-being of others.

Action Items

Integrating faith practices into your daily life allows access to a power beyond you that unleashes the power within you. The practices below offer some places where you can begin:

1. **Delve into the Bible.** If you've never read the Bible and you're up for trying, you'll notice the second that you pick it up that it's a big book with tiny words and thin paper. With that in mind, here are a couple of suggestions:

   - **Start with the book of John.** It's clear, practical, and offers a rich understanding of Jesus, his life, and the principles he embodied.

   - **Follow a reading plan.** This isn't a book of chapters, per se. It's more like a book of books, and they're not necessarily configured to be read in succession, with one flowing nicely into the next. There are many reading plans available, each there to help you read through the Bible in a logical order and in small enough chunks that you can digest what you're reading.

   - **Don't feel pressured to read too much too fast.** Trying to get through the Bible in a hurry can feel like drinking from a fire hose. Consider setting a timer without regard for how far you get. Try and read the Bible for ten to fifteen minutes a day, stopping to reflect as often as necessary, and see how much your life improves.

2. **Consider writing prayers as part of your morning routine.** In prayer and journaling alike, one size does not fit all. Writing prayers plays a regular part in my morning routine, and the reason is that it works for me. It's really no different from writing a letter to a loved one; only my loved one, in this case, is Jesus. It gives me the chance to express my thanks. It lets me write out exactly how I feel, exactly what my needs are in a given season of life. All in all, it helps to clarify my thoughts with myself and with God.

3. **Seek out volunteer opportunities.** There are many ways to volunteer and serve, from local charities to schools to religious organizations. In addition to those avenues, here are some other websites you can check out to find opportunities that match your interests: Volunteermatch.org, Idealist.org, Handsonnetwork.org, Catchafire.org, Serve.gov, and TaprootPlus.org.

The Quiet Call to Your Best

I suggested earlier in the chapter that success is not possible without purpose. I claimed, too, that a lack of purpose ultimately leaves a person empty, longing to be filled by something, anything that will distract from the emptiness. The longing I was referring to is *loud*, like the tantrum of the hungry two-year-old refused a Snickers bar at the check-out line. Many are too willing to heed the tantrums of the ego that demand relief *now*. They carry a feeling of entitlement to immediate gratification through life that keeps them enslaved to an appetite that becomes louder and more persistent the more it is fed. The problem is that Snickers bars are delicious and provide quick relief to the craving, but hunger returns soon after, and satisfying that hunger with *more* Snickers leads eventually to sickness.

It's a trap from which neither the rich nor poor are exempt. Excess money allows the rich unbridled access to the candy store; scarcity produces a longing for relief that ensures the person who races to the candy store every time they have the money will remain poor. They both run on the same treadmill of purpose, where they keep striving for relief that can only come from within.

The longing is loud. It's insistent. The conscience, though, the voice of the Spirit, is soft and patient. It won't shout over the noise or demand to be heard. It also might not tell you what you want to hear. Yes, you want Snickers, but the quieter voice wants your will to be free from the impulses that distract you from pursuing purposes that will provide true nourishment to your spirit.

When you look at a map, you need to know two locations to get to where you need to go: your current location and your destination. Prayer, meditation, and scripture reading provide the quiet and the perspective to perceive both clearly. They unveil the state of your conscience, clarify the things that truly matter to you, and point to the destinations that stir your spirit. Through service and donation, we discover that fulfillment is not found tending to appetites and impulses but to the needs of your brothers and sisters.

As we discovered in chapter two, about three of every four people die with regrets about the things they never set out to accomplish. Why? I think the answer is fear, fear of looking within, fear of believing they are capable of what they hear God whispering that they are meant to be. But all that fades away on the deathbed when the time has run out to listen to our God-given intuition, the restlessness that invites us to look at where we are relative to where we could be. This is why I place worship above all else, because I intend to remain forever open and obedient to the call to my best, the call to live out my mission and die without regrets.

There Is Always Something New to Learn

"If you think education is expensive, try ignorance."

—HOWARD GARDNER

Your mind is the engine that drives all of your plans. Neglect the engine, and you're destined to end up broken down on the side of the road. But not all sources of maintenance nor how you use them are equally beneficial for the upkeep of your engine. Use the wrong oil, and you may damage the engine. Fill it up once and forget it; it'll turn into sludge that no longer does the engine a bit of good. Whether for prevention or correction, it's best to consult the experts to keep your engine running smoothly so it can take you where you need to go reliably.

This brings us to the E in WEALTH: education. Education represents how you maintain your mental fitness and the sharpness of your skills. There are a few reasons why education is imperative. One is that the world is ever-changing, now more than ever, with new technologies and ways of obtaining and transmitting information continuously emerging. Those unwilling to stay afloat with change and learn how to leverage those changes to their benefit are destined to be left behind.

Another is that you willingly waste untold time and energy when you neglect to consult the cheat sheets left by those who withstood the trial and error necessary to attain the insights so you wouldn't have to. Finally, as the previous paragraph suggests, the idle mind is no different from the inactive body; it deteriorates in both form and function without exercise. Education forms new neural pathways, which translates to new abilities that forge new possibilities. When we neglect education, we forgo the awesome opportunity to act as architects of our minds.

In this chapter, I cover the types of education that have played the most important roles in my personal and professional development. I discuss the pros and cons of using books, courses, podcasts, seminars, and coaches and mentors to further your education. In addition, I will touch on how best to use each means of education because, as I said, not all sources nor the ways you use them are equally beneficial for the upkeep of your mind. By the end of this chapter, I want you to have a better idea of how to improve your mind's performance. I want you firing on all cylinders on the road to success.

Books

In 2020, I made it my goal to read a book every week. I accomplished my goal and read fifty-two books that year. It's no coincidence that 2020 turned out to be the year I learned more than any other year of my life. Rewind to my early and midtwenties when I didn't read any books, and my progress was moving at a snail's pace compared to today. The reason? I was trying to build a life without a blueprint. I was bumbling around as an amateur instead of seeking the guidance of pros.

With all the advances in technology and all the shiny new learning methods, books remain a source of learning that is hard to beat. Information comes at us from all angles: YouTube, online courses, podcasts, Investopedia, Tiktok, and TED Talks. The list of learning resources has never been lengthier. But books are the learning resource that have outlived them all and still hasn't gone out of style.

Through books, we have access to the wisdom of the all-stars of our field through the ages. Take *Think and Grow Rich*, the best-selling self-help book of all time with eighty million copies sold, if you're counting. Or how about *How to Win Friends and Influence People*, written by one of the greatest salesmen of all time Dale Carnegie? When we neglect to invest the little time and money necessary to read books like these, books that have stood the test of time and been valuable to so many, we accept naivety over the counsel of the masters and the ripest fruits of their labor. You can't go out and interview Napoleon Hill, and you can't shoot an email over to Dale Carnegie. But luckily, they wrote down their philosophies for you to discover.

Those who claim not to read are doing themselves a great disservice. If you consider time a valuable asset and refuse to read, you are shortchanging yourself. You can waste time recreating the wheel or go straight to the cheat sheet of its creator and sidestep the years of trial and error that led to its established form and function.

I don't necessarily suggest you aim to read fifty-two books in a year as I did. I may have accomplished that goal, but there's a reason I now aim for about half that; along the way, I discovered a book a week is *a lot*. Nevertheless, set your own goal. Make it SMART, make it a priority, and see what happens. Start small but not so small that it doesn't create some accountability and consistency. It takes most people about fifteen minutes to read ten pages. Replace fifteen minutes of mindlessly scrolling through social media with some reading, and you'll have read about twenty books by the end of the year.

But what's most important is the commitment of time. Consider the foolishness of trying to figure out on your own the things others committed years of their lives to learn, the things they deemed so critical that they spent countless hours making sure they were recorded for others to use. Make time to sit at the feet of the pioneers and the modern-day masters. Share in the fruits of all their labor.

Courses

As you now know, I decided a couple of years ago that I wanted to start a YouTube channel and a TikTok. Now anyone who has tried to find success in social media and gain a following of engaged users knows that it can be a dizzying process. It's very easy to get lost in so many channels, formats, algorithms, etc.

So instead of jumping in blindly, I searched diligently for the most reputable courses taught by the most esteemed teachers to find a cheat sheet for success from people who had already aced the test. Sure, I could have stumbled through hours of experimentation and eventually figured it out, but the money I spent on those courses ultimately saved me loads of money. It freed up untold hours so that I could get started sooner and smarter. The result? I applied the lessons I learned from people who had taken the hard, gradual road to success and fast-tracked the growth of my channels. Long story short, I've amassed over a million followers in just a couple of years.

Courses are one of the first sources I turn to when I need to further my education. I mentioned above the unbelievable wealth of information we now have at our fingertips. In years past, we usually had to jump through every hoop leading to a university lecture hall to take a course, and there was a good chance that most of the experience of the person teaching happened within the university walls instead of in the trenches of the industry. The professor pulled their know-how from a textbook, not from their victories and defeats in the actual field.

More and more, expertise is established through effectiveness, not accreditation. When finding a course, I'm looking for someone whose success and character are evident and worth emulating. So it's simple. When I want to learn a new skill, one of the first things I do is seek out a course written by someone I admire, someone who is performing the skill I wish to learn at a high level. When I decided to expand into coaching, for example, I invested in a course on how to structure and deliver an effective coaching program, and the result was Wealthy Investor (WealthyInvestor.com), where I teach students the information and skills I used to find success in real estate investing.

You don't necessarily have to go to college to become an expert in your chosen field. With the internet, you can find the recipe for success straight from someone with their boots on the ground. You can skip all the hypotheticals and the theories and get right to the practical applications. From there, you can test the hypotheses and run the experiments yourself. You can do all this without the need for the certification or accreditation that was required to enter the field in the past.

I'll leave you with two words of advice regarding courses. First, don't let the cost of a course distract you from the potential value of the investment. Let's say a course costs you a thousand bucks, but it contains a blueprint that saves you a year's worth of digging through all the crap to find the gems. If that blueprint leads to a year of growth in three months, would that be worth a thousand dollars?

But don't be impulsive in those investments, either. The flip side of this booming market is that it is undeniably oversaturated, so it calls for some discernment on your part and some legwork on the front end. My advice is to vet their creators and trust your gut. I thoroughly dig through their online presence when deciding which course is right for me. I look at all their free content, such as their YouTube, Instagram,

Twitter, and TikTok. I see what they have to say and whether their message resonates with me.

If you can't find anything, there's a reason for skepticism. You're looking not just to spend your time wisely but also your money, and you're taking a considerable risk if a course is the only trace of a person's voice and message. Be skeptical of those without actual experience. This isn't a university course; with few exceptions, the teacher should practice what they preach.

Podcasts

In 2014, the BiggerPockets podcast opened my eyes to the possibilities that led to my reality today. I was floundering in scarcity, waking up every day to chase money and wishing there was a way of taking advantage of the golden opportunities I saw in real estate investing, opportunities I thought were not available to me given my limited savings at the time. The missing piece was education, and I found it in the BiggerPockets podcast. The information I discovered there equipped me not just with the know-how but also the confidence to move down a path of the others whose journeys were being freely shared there.

Podcasts provided an unstructured, unbound format where ideas were being shared in organic, spontaneous ways that I had not encountered in other learning formats. I was spellbound as I listened to conversations between hosts and guests, bouncing ideas off one another to co-create something entirely new. Essentially, I got to be a fly on the wall, eavesdropping on a casual conversation between renowned individuals about the secrets of their success. Oh, and it was all free.

I stumbled upon the right podcast at the right time, but I was very fortunate. The search for quality podcasts can be dizzying. However, you don't have to carry out your search blindly. Sure, you'll stumble

CHAPTER 11 | THERE IS ALWAYS SOMETHING NEW TO LEARN

upon diamonds in the rough, but pay attention to the charts that organize the episodes by topic and popularity. For me, I seek entrepreneurship, business, or investing episodes. Regardless, these charts can guide you toward the podcasts that most listeners trust. You can take it a step further with reviews, reading through others' reactions and critiques of a show's content to find what is likely to resonate with you.

The advantage of podcasts over courses and physical books is that the format permits consumption while engaging in other activities. Podcasts can add value to the mindless, mundane, and often unavoidable tasks, providing the soundtrack to some leisure pursuits like exercise. I personally listen to podcasts when I'm working out or shooting hoops, and sometimes even during a solo round of golf.

Don't sleep on podcasts like I did for the better half of my twenties. Despite how easy they are to find and consume, the information they freely offer can sometimes change the trajectory of your life completely. That's what Bigger Pockets did for me. For years, I'd been dreaming of finding my way past the velvet rope into the real estate club, and BiggerPockets pulled me out of line and showed me to the back entrance. And if you want to learn how to build wealth that allows you to become rich in all aspects of life, listen to my podcast, *The Wealthy Way Podcast*.

Events

Like all the other means of education covered in this chapter, events provide a rich source of information. The advantages of events over other learning opportunities are twofold. They offer exclusivity and networking.

Typically, an event or conference covers topics geared toward a targeted subject or audience. As a result, you are likely to share many of the goals and aspirations of your fellow attendees. You're likely to share also in their values and interests. Because of this structure, you won't find riper settings for sharing ideas, forming relationships, and planting the seeds of future collaborations.

It's easy to dismiss the value of networking or let discomfort deter you from striking up a conversation with a stranger because you've convinced yourself it won't lead to anything of value. But the value I've gained from connections made at conferences and other similar events is immeasurable. I've done deals with people I met at events. I've joined mastermind groups that led to new friendships and lucrative new collaborations and opportunities.

My advice is to attend events not for the sake of attending, but to go into the experience with the goal of building as many relationships and trading contact information with as many people as possible. So, alongside a goal of how many conferences you will attend, consider setting a goal for how many contacts you'll make at the conference. You might find lifelong friends and allies in business, people who will check in on you, hold you accountable, and, ultimately, make you a better and wealthier person.

Coaches and Mentors

I did not save coaching and mentoring for last by accident. I'll concede right off that this is often the most expensive option but for a good reason. I kept hold of my money for years regarding coaches and mentors. One of the reasons for this is that I lumped all coaches and mentors into the same group as fake gurus who claim expertise without any substance or justification.

So I was defiant. Granted, the BiggerPockets podcast was the invitation I accepted to join the party, and I read everything I could get my hands on after that. But, I stopped there, believing I could save my money and figure it out on my own just fine.

It wasn't until a friend pointed out the irony that I was unwilling to seek out the help of coaches in business despite their incomparable role in my development as an athlete that I stepped back to reconsider my ways. My baseball skills were not honed in isolation. I didn't learn to hit and field by reading books or listening to people talk about swinging and fielding mechanics, but through the feedback of my coaches, who observed my technique and offered corrections, sometimes tiny ones, which led to massive results.

So eventually, I gave it a shot, and it didn't take long for me to realize just how stupid I had been. To make up for my years of stupidity, I hired business coaches, health coaches, and mental coaches. You name it, I did it!

As it turned out, going straight to the source proved the steepest learning curve, the most immediate, efficient, and individualized access to information, and, therefore, the most valuable education I had ever received. Through mentoring and coaching, I had access to an expert who could speak directly to my circumstances, my businesses, my strengths and weaknesses, and my obstacles and opportunities. By spending some real money and hiring coaches and mentors, my companies began to scale to heights that allowed me to pay off those investments countless times over. It put me on the fast track to becoming the person I wanted to be.

Books, podcasts, and seminars can't directly address the issues you face in business and life at any given time. None of these can offer uninterrupted, individualized attention or answers to your most urgent questions as they arise along the journey. In these formats, finding a solution or feedback for my situation requires hours and days, and I'll probably still have unanswered questions.

Once again, I implore those of you who are in your twenties or just starting some venture not to make the same mistake I did. So much time, progress, and money I could have made sooner were wasted on my stubborn determination to figure it out on my own and for free. I now realize how shortsighted it was to delay investing in something that, without a doubt, produced some of my most substantial financial returns.

Action Items

A wealth builder is constantly pushing the boundaries of their mind. Through education, we access the blueprint to move forward efficiently, learning from those who've paved the path themselves through trial and error. Here are some things you can do right away to begin educating yourself:

1. **Get SMART about your regular reading practice.** Keep your accountability firm by being specific about when, where, and how much you commit to reading. If you need help knowing where to start and what might be worth your time, follow me on my Instagram @ryanpineda because reading remains a mainstay of my everyday routine. I keep a running update of what I'm reading in the story highlights of my page, complete with reviews and recaps. If it's great, I'll say so, and if it sucks, you know I'll tell you!

2. **Speak to the speakers.** Typically, a conference will offer the option of a VIP rate, which may include access to the speakers themselves, and, yes, I realize this may be viewed as a luxury to those less financially fortunate. However, I will simply offer you this thought: a VIP ticket can become an unthinkably high-yield investment based upon what you stand to gain from meeting high-level professionals in your field. So, if you can't afford the VIP ticket, use your boldness and ingenuity to figure out a way to gain backstage access or the ear of those speaking. Often, one connection or piece of advice from a person of that stature can change the trajectory of your life.

3. **Get a coach or mentor.** I fully recognize that budgetary considerations are real and should not be ignored when choosing a coach. But, there are wise ways to find a mentor or coach who can be an incredible source of information and support, even if the person doesn't have a lot of notoriety. Let's say your dream coach is Warren Buffett. You'll need to get creative unless you have a few million dollars of disposable income. But Warren Buffet has employees. Warren Buffet has trained people and mentored people as well. They may not be the legend himself, but they're easier to access, cost less, and probably more familiar with the issues *you* face each day.

Improving on the Wheel

You may have noticed a pattern here. Books played an incredible role in my path to success. I've since gone on to share the story of my own path through this book and the one I wrote a few years back, *Flip Your Future*. I turned to courses created by experts to determine the best way forward on multiple endeavors, from coaching to social media, and eventually created my own courses to show others how I did it. I became so convinced of the value of podcasts that I started my own podcast, *The Ryan Pineda Show*, which would become what is now the *Wealthy Way Podcast*. I regularly speak at seminars. I created *Wealthy Investor Coaching* and even a program called *Golf with Ryan* to offer others the incredible value I received from guidance and mentorship.

Essentially, I set out to create the educational resources I wish I had had quick access to when I started. Once you're done reading this book, I urge you to check them out. They represent what I learned when I invested my time and money and, even more importantly, what I've learned by applying them in the real world.

Obviously, my podcasts are free, and there is a library of YouTube, TikTok, and Instagram content to guide you along your path. Of course, there are products and services I offer that will require a financial investment in your education.

What I hope you take away is the unmatched opportunity represented by the money invested in your education. The tools I've covered here will save you time and make you money. They'll connect you with new friends and business associates. The resources I offer are a few among countless others. When it came to my education, I let skepticism and stinginess stand in the way of opportunity for far too long. I hope you will take the advice and resources I've offered to seize those opportunities sooner.

CHAPTER 12

Put Your Money to Work

"It's not how much money you make, but how much money you keep, how hard it works for you, and how many generations you keep it for."

—ROBERT KIYOSAKI

I've spent a lot of time in this book arguing that true wealth extends *beyond* financial wealth. And while money is just one aspect of true wealth, it is nevertheless one that should not be neglected. Handled and leveraged responsibly, money facilitates freedom. It grants flexibility with your time and your choices. It creates the opportunity to invest in assets that further grow your income, and it can facilitate the freedom to pursue wealth in the other areas of your life because, let's face it, everything costs money.

Healthy foods cost more than unhealthy foods, and good luck getting into a gym without a membership. Want an education beyond what you can find on YouTube? You're going to have to pay up. That vacation will have to wait until you have more money coming in than going out. Maybe you want to use your earnings to help others by donating to causes. The more you bring in, the more you can hand out.

True, money won't buy happiness, at least not directly. But you can use your money in ways that affirm your values and strengthen your resolve. You can use it to expand the reach of your skills and your influence.

Build Your Foundation

Lebron James earned the name "King James" not because of his elite legislative skills but because he has held court on the hardwood for the past twenty years. He may well sit at the end of the bench when it comes to his artistic abilities or his carpentry skills, but the fact is that none of those things matter. In the same way, a quick Google image search of Leonardo DiCaprio spending a day at the beach will reveal that he is no health and fitness guru, but his fitness as an actor is unmatched. DiCaprio and Lebron are case studies in the first principle of affluence that I will cover: when you're the absolute master of one skill, you make yourself invaluable.

Bruce Lee summed up this philosophy of success like this: "I fear not the man who has practiced 10,000 kicks once, but I fear the man who has practiced one kick 10,000 times." In essence, he was advocating the relationship between focused practice and mastery. He was also warning against dabbling mindlessly, never really setting a firm intention to commit to a path that will lead to change in the skills that will eventually lead to changes in your opportunities and circumstances.

Couch flipping is an example from my own life. There was a time when I turned all of my attention toward being the best in that venture. Sharpening my skill in finding and turning a deal was the kick I practiced ten thousand times, and as a result, I became a master and carried that into everything that came after.

I parlayed my dealmaking prowess into success as a house flipper. Through that, I took on new skills and knowledge of the real estate industry that I carried into starting and leading businesses, delegating their moving parts to those whose focus had made them masters in those areas. The real kicker is that I would also go on to make YouTube and TikTok videos sharing the secrets behind my success in couch flipping that have been viewed by millions.

I couldn't have skipped any of the steps that brought me to where I am today, and it all started in the trenches of dealmaking. Eventually, I saw an opportunity in social media. It was a platform where I could offer something of value, share my skills and knowledge, and gain exposure for my businesses. There was a context where the skills I practiced so diligently to find success in couch flipping provided the foundation of the content I made available. Through courses and mentors, and lots of practice, I built another skill base in content creation around the one that paved the path to all the others.

While Lebron showed up day after day at dawn to sharpen his skills as a basketball player, I learned to recognize and seize upon a deal. We both built a kingdom on the foundation of our core skills. So the takeaway is to start from the beginning by cultivating your core money-making skill. You may not like everything about it, and it may not be something that you want to see yourself doing long-term (that was certainly the case with me when I began couch flipping) but develop something that you can bank on and build upon with other skills as the changing circumstances and opportunities dictate.

Side Hustles

A side hustle is any job or occupation that brings in *extra* money beyond one's regular job and main source of income. The key word here is extra. The categories of side hustles are numerous and growing every day. What you choose to do and how often you choose to do it is a matter of your skills, the lifestyle you desire, and the amount of work you are willing and able to put in.

If you're disgruntled with the career path you're on or lost about what to do with your life, you don't necessarily have to abandon your current post outright, but you should begin considering and experimenting with other ways of making money and honing your skills in your free time, no matter how short that time may be. A side hustle allows you a testing ground where you step into something new and take bold but calculated risks to determine how potentially lucrative it could be. Having some "extra money" may be an adequate justification, but anything worth doing is worth doing well, especially if you are less than happy with your current lifestyle.

But a word of warning: what you intend as a side hustle may well become your main gig. That certainly turned out to be the case with me. I started couch flipping, intending to make an extra thousand dollars per month. But it wasn't long before I realized that I was capable of making much more, enough to hang my hat on. Well, the money I made from that became not my primary source of income but also served as the investment money I would use to buy into the game I'd wanted to play all along, house flipping.

The point is, I didn't realize when I decided to invest in a little experiment with buying and selling couches how much more I'd get than I had bargained for. In a million years, I couldn't have anticipated the bargain that my investment would turn out to be.

Your Personal Brand

The impression you project to others, whether through face-to-face interactions or social media posts, comprises your personal brand. So unless you're sitting around in your pajamas all day interacting with no one, your personal brand is continually being formed and put on display.

It is important to understand that few things are more important to keep in mind regarding business. This will only become more critical as time goes on. Social media isn't going anywhere. The metaverse will become more mainstream, allowing users to play and work in 3D augmented realities. Your brand will only become more visible as these technologies take hold.

Your personal brand is critical to business because people want to minimize risk in choosing who to work with. They want to eliminate unknowns. They want to know who you are and what you stand for before they commit any of their time or money to you.

Consider the example of real estate. A couple looking for the help of an agent to find a new home in an unfamiliar market will likely perform a Google search and find many options. Who do you think they will choose? Lisa, who posts regular social media content that demonstrates her expertise in real estate, or Zack, whose only available information is a phone number and address?

Barring some strange coincidence like the couple's affection for dudes named Zack, they're probably going to opt for Lisa, who is intentional in her demonstration of who she is and what she's about. They're probably going to look further into Lisa's online presence and find that she has an Instagram, a Facebook, TikTok, and YouTube videos. They're going to see that she's active in her field, and they're going to want to be a part of that.

Putting yourself out there builds trust because it makes you known. Someone like Lisa seeks to put her best foot forward, sharing her commitment to her clients, enthusiasm about the homes she lists, excitement for the homes she's sold, and glowing testimonials of the people she represents. Over the last couple of years, I have learned that word of mouth is no longer adequate. I believe there was no more profitable decision that I have made than choosing to take my brand seriously and cultivating it through my social media presence.

Based on observation and first-hand experience, my philosophy is this: it's not always the best product or business that wins. It's the best marketer. So market yourself. You don't have to produce at the rate I do. You don't have to have a studio or expensive equipment. But aim to have *some* online presence, some profile that answers a potential client's number one question: Who is this person, and why should I entrust my hard-earned money to their service? Your job is to make the answer to that question readily and widely available and to make sure it's engaging, generous, and authentic enough to instill trust in those who ask the question.

Not only has my presence on social media and my attention to building my brand attracted customers and, in turn, generated revenue, but it has also attracted nearly every employee I work with now. While others spend money on recruiting through job ads and recruiters, invest time and lose money on interviews and reviewing stacks of resumes, I get proposals from those who know and believe in what I'm up to, want to be involved, and believe in their ability to contribute. My investment in media has turned out to be one of the most potent I have ever made, more than I ever anticipated, strengthening my business and growing my income by leaps and bounds.

Investments

Bruce Lee had the right idea regarding investing, too—diversification is good, but it should take a back seat to specialization. Consider the portfolios of some of the most successful investors. Warren Buffett specializes in stocks. Venture capitalist Bill Gurley leveraged his expertise in startup culture to invest in eventual behemoths like Uber, Stitch Fix, and Nextdoor. I specialize in real estate.

The importance of mastering one skill or understanding all the ins and outs of one context also applies to investing. Granted, I hold some investments outside of real estate, but not without consulting with experts I know and trust. I also own businesses and depend on people with skills in areas I know very little about. In both cases, I delegate that portion of my strategy to others with that expertise.

But like your core skills, the quality of your investments depends largely on consistency and staying up-to-date with the market. Don't forget, Bruce Lee also said, "Be like water." You have to remain flexible, doing your homework and learning through the means covered in chapter eleven so you can adapt to the changes in the playing field and know the rules of the game.

Along with consulting with experts, there's also the option of investing in another individual's deals, something I have facilitated through my company Pineda Capital (PinedaCapital.com). Seeing the success I have enjoyed in real estate, many began to ask if there were opportunities to invest in bigger deals than I could afford with just my money, deals like the 300-unit apartment complex we purchased as part of our first deal. But a variety of professionals, like doctors and business owners, fully immersed in their fields without experience in the real estate business, can benefit from my real estate investment knowledge to make money alongside their main gig.

The overarching point is simple: don't be careless or haphazard with your hard-earned money. Don't bet on chances that can be mitigated through education. When a crash course in some investment area isn't feasible, give your money to someone who has done the legwork already, whether that be an expert in that field, a financial planner, or a fund manager.

Taxes

More income means more taxes, right? Well, without a strategy, that may well be true. But play your cards right, and you may make millions without giving a dime back—and I would know. Real estate investing is one of the best ways to minimize tax liability.

Robert Kiyosaki says, "Employees pay the highest percentage of taxes. Big business and investors pay the least." And he's right. A W-2 employee gets the worst tax benefits out of anyone in the country. For better or worse, those who get the best treatment in terms of taxes are business owners and real estate investors.

Through investing in real estate, I enjoy passive income and appreciation of my assets year after year. Not only that, but I can pay down the principal balance of the loan for a rental property through the payments I receive from its tenants.

But perhaps the biggest perk to real estate, which is less obvious from an outside perspective, is the tax benefits resulting from depreciation. Depreciation is the projected dollar amount required for the upkeep of a property, an amount that can be deducted from your taxes even if you haven't spent the money on maintenance yet! The total is then deducted from the income generated through that property. So long story short, own enough properties, and that write-off could potentially amount to paying *nothing* in taxes—zero!

Business owners enjoy similar advantages. Many of your expenses can be filed as write-offs as a business owner. For example, I don't have to pay taxes on the computer I'm using to write this book because it's being used to help me make money. If I were a W-2 employee, that would not be an option.

Here you have another benefit to starting a side hustle. By doing a side hustle, you are technically a business owner. Therefore, anything you may purchase to improve your performance and the profits produced by your side hustle is fair game for a write-off.

In fact, I leveraged my interest in this topic and my desire to guide others toward avoiding unnecessary taxation by starting my own CPA business, TrueBooks (truebookscpa.com). We help hundreds of busy real estate investors and business owners maintain proper books and execute the right strategies throughout the year to save them as much time and money as possible come tax time. If you opt to use my company or another CPA, you want to ensure that they are highly knowledgeable in areas like depreciation, business expenses, side hustles, and all the other ways you can minimize what you end up paying on the back end.

In advocating for financial literacy in tax law, Kiyosaki also said, "It's not about how much money you make, but about how much money you keep." You keep more money by having a good tax strategy, so either set out to educate yourself or hand it off to the experts.

Debt

There are many so-called financial gurus, especially ones in the Christian world, who view debt, any debt, as inherently evil. They say to never take out loans, even for a house or a car. Don't use credit cards. End of story. For example, a quick search of Dave Ramsey's website for advice on credit card usage brings up an article entitled, "Ready to Take the Next Step? (Hint: it involves a pair of scissors.)"

Others like Robert Kiyosaki and Grant Cardone take a more flexible view, suggesting you discriminate between good and bad debt and take on only the former.[34][35] "Good debt," in their perspective, is debt taken on to make you money. Real estate, for example, would fall into this category since it creates passive income.

The problem with the hardliners like Dave Ramsey is that they throw the baby out with the bathwater. Yes, some people lack financial savvy or impulse control, and credit cards might be bad for those people. But for the individual who exercises discipline and calculates the risk behind their actions, refusing to utilize loans under any

---

34 Robert Kiyosaki, "Rich Dad Poor Dad" (Scottsdale: Plata Publishing, 1997).

35 Grant Cardone, *"How to Create Wealth Investing in Real Estate: How to Build Wealth with Multi-Family Real Estate"* (Aventura: Cardone Training Technologies, Incorporated, 2018).

circumstances can be downright irresponsible. It's self-sabotage by passing up sensible risks with potentially massive upsides to remain firmly and idly planted on some imagined moral high ground.

If I had taken to the view that credit card debt is evil, I wouldn't have gotten started in real estate when I did. I may still be pinching pennies trying to save enough money to buy entry into the game, watching others make millions off loan-financed homes that doubled and tripled in value over the past decade. If I had taken Dave Ramsey's advice, I would still be struggling, saving for probably a decade to get to the position of buying a single property. Instead, I've soared past one investment property and now buy hundreds of units yearly.

But, you know the story. I committed the cardinal sin: I maxed out our credit cards. The fact is that money funded my entry into the house-flipping business, the one that changed my life, my family's life, the lives of those I employ, the ones I teach, all the way down to those I donate a significant proportion of my wealth to. I could go on. Bottom line, there is never a day when I regret that decision and wish I had not taken on the debt that pales laughably compared to what it produced.

You will be hard-pressed to find a business or investment where borrowing didn't play a role in generating future money. The advice that all debt is inherently bad is becoming increasingly outdated, particularly regarding the real estate market. If you had been trying to save up to buy in cash over those five to ten years, you missed out on a massive opportunity. You can still get a conventional loan, but you would've been better off putting 3 percent down earlier. Then ride the appreciation upward versus trying to save 20 percent and missing out on the gains.

Despite what Dave Ramsey will have you believe, you don't have to put your life on hold until you have the cash in hand. You aren't doomed if you take the calculated risk of taking on debt for the sake of a can't-miss deal. Deciding whether to take on debt is less about low or high interest and good or evil than answering the question: How will I use it?

The Bible says much about being a good steward with the money you are entrusted with, and you can and should take the same approach in your attitude toward debt. Are you taking it on because you want to look and feel cool by buying a car you can't afford? Pump the brakes. But maybe you want that same loan to get a car to rent out on Turo and make money? In that case, you are beginning to get the right idea.

Ultimately it's up to you to be honest with yourself. What are your motives? What constitutes a need versus a want, an asset versus a liability? Start with responsibility. If you don't have that figured out, you're not ready to take on debt.

Action Items

Although money comprises just one aspect of the Wealthy Way, you must understand how to make money work for you. The following are some ways you can begin to improve your financial intelligence right away:

1. **Identify and cultivate your core money-making skill.** We discussed the many available avenues for enhancing your knowledge and skills in chapter eleven. Consider these means of investing in the skill that you see as your greatest asset. Also, consider taking a second job or side hustle that exercises this skill. In this way, you will not only bring in extra money but also increase your earning potential for the future.

2. **Get clear on your online brand and content strategy.** This is a perfect opportunity to incorporate some free writing into your morning journaling routine to think about what you want to project in the things you post online. Who is your target audi-

ence? Are there online personalities or brands you admire and would like to emulate? What do you want your audience to do with the things you post, i.e., what do you want to accomplish? To help entrepreneurs build their brands and create content, I started a company called Wealthy Creator (WealthyCreator.io).

3. **Reconsider your debt strategy.** Assuming you carry some debt, take an inventory of where you have invested the money you have borrowed. This will tell you all you need to know about your motives and the level of responsibility you bring to the decision to borrow. Are you investing in assets that produce cash flow? Then, double down on your education to further develop your knowledge in whatever investment area you choose to specialize in. Swiping your AMEX to buy luxuries with money you don't have? Then, I'd suggest you visit the website ramseysolutions.com for advice on your next steps.

The Wealthy's Ways

Certain qualities distinguish the wealthy from the middle and lower class. The rich often possess signature skills, like a kick practiced ten thousand times over, that set them apart from all others and ensure they will remain indispensable. They also tend to be more intentional in projecting these and other skills. They consider the image they project as their brand and recognize that by enhancing public perception, they also boost their earning potential. On the other hand, those who are less well off are more likely to be haphazard in their cultivation of skills and how they promote themselves if they do so.

The wealthy often demonstrate greater willingness than others to experiment with alternatives to their primary means of income, not hesitating to poke and prod for the possibility of striking oil elsewhere. When one source of income crashes and burns or a secondary source of income becomes more lucrative than the first, they are in a position to pivot. They have options.

The differences in investments, debt and taxes, primarily come down to education. The wealthy apply discernment informed by deep knowledge of a field to stack the odds in their favor or turn to someone who can before placing their bets. Whether money is spent or borrowed, they take on risks, but always calculated ones, usually for assets that are less subject to taxation and more likely to generate additional income. Those with less are more likely to spend by necessity or with less intention. Either they don't have money to invest, or they mindlessly heed the advice to "diversify" when they could put their money into areas they understand. They take on debt impulsively rather than strategically, necessarily instead of voluntarily. They borrow money to buy things they neither need nor can afford with whatever money is leftover after taxes.

Of course, money facilitates freedom just as lack can restrict it. But developing your skills and your brand, making informed choices in the way you invest and borrow, understanding taxes: these are choices we have the freedom to make. It is not difficult to see why the rich get richer, and the poor get poorer, but often, it comes down to knowing the common factors that underlie affluence and using what freedom we have to invest our time and energy into educating ourselves to leverage them to our favor.

CHAPTER 13

How, Then, Shall You Live

"Learn to be happy with what you have
while you pursue all that you want."

—JIM ROHN

C an money buy happiness? This can seem like a silly question for those whose income can't keep up with their expenses. As the thinking goes, everything would change if they could hit the lottery or suddenly acquire a massive inheritance from a distant relative.

But the truth, according to science, is a little more nuanced than that. A 2021 study by Matthew Killingsworth demonstrated that a certain amount of money certainly helps to ensure a happy existence.[36] Anything below seventy-five thousand a year and a person is destined to a degree of struggle that will impact their emotional well-being. But the increase in happiness once they've exceeded that income

---

36 Matthew Killingsworth, "Experienced well-being rises with income, even above $75,000 per year." *Proceedings of the National Academy of Sciences* 118, no. 4 (2021): e2016976118.

starts to flatten out. In fact, for most, there is no difference at all once they've reached the two hundred thousand dollar mark.

Once you have reached a level of income that provides for your needs and leaves some room for spending, what matters most is how you choose to live and spend your money. A 2011 study out of Harvard demonstrated that money spent on experiences offered more life satisfaction than money spent on material things.[37] They also found that money spent for the benefit of others led to greater happiness than that spent selfishly. All in all, the purchases that affirmed a person's values, not the ones that boosted their egos, led to lasting happiness.

That brings us to the next attribute of WEALTH: lifestyle. Here, we introduce the concept of margin, that critical buffer area where one's choices ultimately dictate whether they'll lead a life of satisfaction or disappointment. We will examine the concept of margin as it relates to time and money, encouraging you to leave enough room to live and choose freely and make choices that will provide you a life worth living.

Margin

More often than not, feeling stressed or overwhelmed comes down to insufficient margin. The simplest way to describe margin is the difference between what you have and what you need. It's not how much money you have. It's not how much time you have. It's the margin that you leave in the supply of those resources. Once that margin closes, like the needle closing in on the redline of a speedometer, stress and overwhelm are the result. When that supply is small, your demand for relief is high.

---

37 Dunn, Elizabeth W., Daniel T. Gilbert, and Timothy D. Wilson. "If money doesn't make you happy, then you probably aren't spending it right." *Journal of Consumer Psychology* 21, no. 2 (2011): 115-125.

A person who brings in one hundred thousand in income and has one hundred thousand in expenses has no margin in money and, therefore, no margin for error. They're vulnerable to whatever unexpected expense will take them from no margin to a negative margin, and there are plenty of case studies among pro athletes to illustrate that having mountains of money does not necessarily equate to a deep valley of margin. As you might have figured out by now, another word for negative margin is debt, and the only ways to get out of debt are to make more than you spend or spend less than you earn —and this is where lifestyle comes into play.

If you are living with no financial margin, you need to either downgrade your lifestyle or upgrade your income. It's as simple as that. Maybe it's time to trade that luxury car for an economy. Perhaps it's time to opt out of a few steak dinners and cook rice and beans at home instead.

Or maybe you love your lifestyle too much to cut back, in which case your only sensible option is to figure out a way to bring in enough additional income to outpace your spending. Is there a side hustle that aligns with your skills and interests? Is it time to use your extra time to look for a new career altogether? Make a new investment? Double your income, and suddenly the same one hundred thousand you're spending that had Dave Ramsey wagging his finger at you will have him singing your praises.

When my wife and I were first married, we spent something in the ballpark of three thousand per month. That number has probably increased tenfold and yet the margin has remained the same. My expenses increased following increases in my earnings, not vice versa.

The relationship between margin and stress extends beyond money, with time being the most obvious. There's a subculture of entrepreneurs who pride themselves on how many hours they work, how few hours they sleep, or do anything outside their "hustle." "I'll rest when I'm dead," they say. So they use up all their margin on work and redline everything else when they forgo rest. But what's the point of amassing money and still being completely overwhelmed? What kind of husband, wife, sibling, or friend do you think these people are?

The way I see it, if I wake at six in the morning and go to bed at eleven, that leaves me seventeen hours. I spend the first four on my morning routine, and then I work from ten until five in the evening, which leaves me six additional hours of margin that I can invest in the people I love.

The principles for supply and demand of margin don't apply to time in the same way as money. As I've reiterated time and again, the reason I place such value on time is that it's non-renewable and non-refundable. Want to have more time for family and leisure? Well, you have twenty-four hours to spend whether your net worth number has four or nine zeros behind it. Sure, you can sleep less, but guess what? There's a margin for energy: your energy for your spiritual and emotional well-being, your family, and, yes, even the energy you have for your work. Trying to bargain with the margins of your time and energy is a losing proposition and a recipe for ravaged health and wasted wealth. Your only option for margin when it comes to your time is to trade working harder for working smarter.

Budgeting

Most are familiar with budgeting in its simplest form: incoming on the left, outgoing on the right, and voilà—there, you have a budget. One of the more popular philosophies on budgeting proposes that you live on 80 percent of your income, save or invest 10 percent, and give the remaining 10 percent to a cause. This represents a sensible approach to money management for most of the population, but for those on the higher end of the income bracket, making a million and spending eight hundred thousand hardly seems sensible. In fact, it is not uncommon among the very wealthy to live on less than 10 percent of their income. There's only so much you can buy.

As a Christian, I think about how much I want to give first, then how much I want to save and invest. What's left over is what I spend. Most people spend their money first, and if there's anything left over, that's what they give, save, and invest. You need to reverse the order.

Regardless of income, a truly robust budget consists of four categories, not just two. To compose a budget that takes lifestyle into account entirely requires that you answer four questions:

- How much are you going to spend?

- How much will you save?

- How much will you invest?

- How much will you give?

When it comes to budgeting, there are two types of people: earners and savers. The way that these categories are allocated will vary depending on which type of person is creating the budget.

The primary focus of the saver is on the outgoing category. In their view, living within one's means equates to saving more by spending less. It comes down to lowering expectations, setting aside desires, and delaying gratification until there is a large enough stockpile to proceed without debt–or forever, if necessary.

On the other hand, the primary focus of the earner is on the incoming category. They are less focused on living within their means than expanding the means they have to live within. They don't lower expectations or set aside desires. Instead, they use them as their benchmark for earning what's necessary to lead the lifestyle they wish. So, the former favors self-restraint while the latter encourages ingenuity.

I, for one, wish I had stopped being a saver and started being an earner sooner. All too often, I think savers impede their creativity and underestimate their ingenuity by conceding defeat to the limitations imposed by the incoming column of their budget. Again, certain public figures argue for the nobility of penny-pinching to financial freedom or to the grave, whichever comes first. But a saver's mentality will not lead to getting rich quickly, which has an unfairly bad reputation.

Time spent preoccupied with saving is lost on focusing on ways of increasing earning power. I am not suggesting that there is anything wrong with living within your means, but making that your primary focus suffocates creativity, which is the driver of your ability to earn much more. It's self-handicapping to obsess about a five-dollar coffee instead of thinking about how to make a hundred extra bucks to make that five dollars a moot point.

So while savers ask: "What do I need to cut out in my life?" Earners consider: "What do I need to do differently to attain what I want in life?" My approach today goes like this: This is the lifestyle I want to live, with this type of house, this type of car, this vacation, donating this amount of money—how can I have *all* of that? My mentality is that there is a way to do it all; I just have to find it. Your income is not capped unless you assent to it being that way.

Again, I am not suggesting that you live beyond your current means. As I said, I have always maintained a margin. But I also discourage you from muzzling your desires for more things or nicer things, living like a miser until you've saved enough to live out your elderly years in decrepit luxury. Instead, know your current ratios and look to the lifestyle you wish to lead as the starting point for what you need to earn to live on a smaller chunk of your income while giving, saving, and investing more.

How Lavish?

How lavish do you want to live? Do you want a Ford or a Ferrari? A mobile home or a mansion? As I said, I am not a proponent of suppressing your desires. But the first thing you should do in making these decisions is to determine the amount you can spend that will allow you to maintain a comfortable margin of expenses to income.

If, for example, you have ten thousand dollars in addition to the margin you have decided is acceptable, then the next step is to determine where that stands with the things you want to buy. So essentially, you need to put your wants in order of their priority. Maybe you're into cars or watches. Like me, maybe you get a sense of gratification from eating at nice restaurants with your significant other. Consider those things alongside your tolerance for margin when making decisions on how to allocate your money.

Think of your money as an investment in your happiness, and be honest about your motives. Don't buy a Rolex watch if it's not ultimately going to bring you a deep sense of satisfaction or if it will narrow your margin to the point of feeling overwhelmed. Either scenario is a shortsighted and irresponsible way to spend your money. Are you interested in buying something because it's an authentic expression of yourself? Is this something that aligns with your best self or one that makes you feel superior to someone else? If you're buying something to project a false image or to keep up with someone else, then you can rest assured it will not bring you fulfillment. That satisfaction lasts only as long as you can uphold the facade or until someone with something better inevitably comes along.

Speaking of satisfaction, don't neglect experiences. Some discount the value of experiences because they are intangible and can't be held in hand or sold for profit. I believe these are narrow-minded views. The memories you take from your experiences don't lose value. They won't break or wear out or go out of style. Sooner or later, the

Lamborghini will break down. It's going to lose its luster in comparison to the new model. Before long, its novelty will be lost on you and become your new norm. So take that vacation and stay in that fancy hotel. The memories will remain at the end of your story long after the Lambo's broken down and the Rolex has lost its shine.

Action Items

Wealth Builders decide the kind of lifestyle they desire and set about making it happen from there. Here are some ways you can arrive at the point that you're living the life you want on less while saving, giving, and investing more:

1. **Design your lifestyle.** This is the time to dream big. This is the time to set aside your inhibitions and self-doubt and dream big. If you imagine living your best life a year or five years from now, what are you driving? Where are you living? What vacations are you taking? This is the starting point before moving to action item two.

2. **Become an earner by asking: How can I afford it?** In *Rich Dad Poor Dad*, Robert Kiyosaki explains that his rich dad would not allow Robert to speak the words he heard his dad often say: I can't afford it. Instead, he encouraged the alternative: How can I afford it? He told Robert that those words "opened up the brain and forced it to think and search for answers." So think about the "what" of lifestyle first and the "how" of earning it second.

3. **Pay yourself first.** Another key lesson Kiyosaki's rich dad shared was to "pay yourself first." Kiyosaki's book discusses the importance of tending to your assets and investments before turning your attention to bills. I propose you apply the same philosophy to the use of time. When you make your schedule, first fill in your time-bound appointments and obligations (i.e.,

your work schedule, meetings, your daughter's dance recital, etc.). From there, "pay yourself" by scheduling activities that affirm your values and your desired lifestyle. For example, set a firm appointment for that workout, complete with time and location, and treat it with the same level of accountability as you would a commitment made to someone else.

Lifestyle in the Margins

When you step back and look at what brings about daily contentment, how you spend your time matters more than your possessions or the number of zeros in your bank account balance. Ultimately, it is your lifestyle that gives meaning to life. There will be uneasiness in the spirit of the man who desires to be a good husband and father but leaves no margin for his family in his life. There will be restlessness for the woman who values her fitness but makes no time for exercise.

When it comes to budgeting time for the areas of your life that matter most to you, the principles are no different from those that relate to budgeting money. You must first take an honest look at how much time you want to spend on each area of your life. How much do you want to work on a daily and weekly basis? How much time do you want to spend with your family? How often and for how long do you want to work out? From there, you turn to your current schedule and determine whether the available margin of time allows for their fulfillment or whether you need to make changes to free up the time to live your desired lifestyle.

Of course, some jobs place unavoidable constraints on how much control you have over that margin. If you're working from eight in the morning to six at night, the reality is you only have a few hours to work with unless you want to forgo sleep and sacrifice your well-being. In this situation, you have to prioritize some activities and, in the process, eliminate others to accommodate what you value most.

Either that or you need to use the time you have left to change your circumstances to gain more control over your schedule. Maybe you try a side hustle a few hours or days a week to determine whether it proves more flexible and adequately lucrative for you to leave your current job. Maybe you set aside an hour to write a proposal for remote work to your boss so that you can work more in less time.

There's an interesting paradox when it comes to ensuring that we make time for the things we value. When the boss tells us to come in at eight in the morning and leave at six in the evening, or a friend asks us to meet for dinner at seven, we demonstrate our commitment by showing up on time. We'll clear out everything so we don't let that person down. We innately understand the importance of reliability in our commitments to others. Yet, our commitment too often wavers when it comes to showing up for the things that matter to us or even bothering to schedule them in the first place. Contentment doesn't happen by accident, and it doesn't happen without commitment. Ultimately, your contentment comes down to what happens in the margins.

CHAPTER 14

Who's on Your Side?

"When life on earth is ending, people don't surround themselves
with objects. What we want around us is people—
people we love and have relationships with."

—RICK WARREN

I t's scientifically proven that people with strong relationships live
more fulfilling lives—they are less prone to anxiety and depression, have higher self-esteem, and are overall more satisfied with
their lives.[38] They heal faster, sleep better, and live longer. No matter how many times and in how many ways researchers examine the
effects of social connections, the results are the same: if you don't have
healthy relationships, you won't be happy with your life.[39] There is no
way around it, and no amount of success in your career or money in
your bank account can change that. Strong relationships don't just
make you happier and healthier. They also bring about qualities that

---

38 Debra Umberson and Jennifer Karas Montez. "Social relationships and health: A flashpoint
for health policy." *Journal of Health and Social Behavior* 51, no. 1__suppl (2010): S54-S66.

39 Saphire-Bernstein, Shimon, and Shelley E. Taylor. "Close relationships and happiness."
Oxford handbook of happiness (2013).

increase the likelihood of developing stronger social connections: greater empathy and the ability to trust and cooperate with others.

Of course, the opposite is true of those who neglect relationships in their lives. The payoff for a serial hustler who brags about a seventy-hour workweek is likely to be a deep sense of unfulfillment. They spend all their time stroking their own ego and building their bank account but have no one to share it with. They don't bother demonstrating that they value the people around them and wonder why all that work and money hasn't changed the loneliness they expected it would.

If you don't invest in the success of your relationships, then I would argue that you can't find true success. For that reason, this chapter will discuss each category of individuals who comprise the T in WEALTH—your team.

Family

Never was I more acutely aware of the importance of family in my life than during James's tumultuous first year. If ever my commitment was in question, it was then—first with his arrival, two months early and two months before he was ready to venture outside the nourishment and safety of the womb, and again when a fall nearly negated a year of progress we had struggled to attain. Granted, family had always played a central role in my life, but it was an aspect of life I had the good fortune to assume would always progress smoothly.

But January of 2019, when James was born, marked a turning point in my perspective and priorities. James needed me. Mindy needed me. I innately understood business to be subordinate to family. My primary and unconditional commitment belonged to them.

Since then, life has resumed much of its smoothness and predictability. It would be easy for me to fall back into the mindset I had before James's birth, but the promises I made to myself then are no less true or critical than they were during that time of such upheaval. My family still needs me.

To ensure that I don't fall into complacency, I have established a certain set of rules and boundaries that assure that I don't neglect the importance of family in my life. I will not work weekends. Others may view the weekend as an opportunity to catch up on what they didn't get to or get ahead on what's to come. I don't leave myself that option. I treat weekends as time for my family, and I treat that as a sacred and nonnegotiable commitment. The same goes for my businesses and the employees I've hired to work there. I do one better than Chick-fil-A; the office is closed Saturday *and* Sunday. I want everyone to live out the benefits of spending time with their families.

There are a few additional rules. I leave the office by five o'clock, and I'm home for dinner with the family each and every night. Every Friday is date night—no kids, no friends, just us, enjoying the absurd wealth of food and entertainment that Vegas offers. This is the time for Mindy and me to be completely present with one other and reconnect after our busy weeks.

Far from taking time and value away from work, I firmly believe these commitments have made me *more* productive and successful. When I return to work on a Monday morning, I am recharged and enjoy a clear conscience and perspective on why I am putting in the work.

Fortunately for me, even my business is a family affair. My value for my sister, for example, goes beyond our bond as siblings. In business, she is my right-hand woman who oversees all the companies I own. Of course, we spend a lot of time together, but our trust grows from the value we place on family. We have each other's back, and as a result, our success is reciprocal.

My parents also play a role in ensuring everything runs smoothly. My dad helps with project management. I make an investment, and he ensures the work that goes into getting it to market happens effectively and promptly. And, of course, my mom's thirty years of real estate experience also means she's there to help me find the deals that keep my real estate business thriving.

The result is a work life that does not interfere with my family life because I have worked to keep them intertwined. We spend a lot of time together, and our bond as family members extends to our shared goals as business partners.

I am not claiming to be perfect or suggesting you have to be. Yes, I aspire to leave the office by five each night, and I usually do, but sometimes I am late. There are weekends when I have to go on business trips or attend speaking engagements. Sometimes I'm not in the office but am preoccupied with work or answering "urgent" calls that could really be left for the next day. I'm obviously not giving my family my full presence at those times.

Nevertheless, the goals remain. They are the anchor I return to when I go off track. I believe you should have anchors too. You need to take the value you have for your family and translate that into concrete goals and intentions on how to cultivate those relationships. There will be distractions. There will be days when you just don't feel like it. But you have to affirm its value through persistent action.

Friends

I am very fortunate to still be friends with many of the people I met in my twenties, a stage of my life that looked dramatically different from what it does today. At that time, my day-to-day existence looked far more similar to my old friends' lives than it does today. Certainly, most are happy and successful, but I can't say that any of them spend their days producing YouTube videos for millions of viewers every day. Though my love for those friends has not changed, our paths and priorities eventually diverged completely.

There is a saying that you are the average of the five people you hang out with the most. If I was the average of my friends in my twenties, that wasn't a bad thing by any means, but it wasn't going to prepare me for success on my path. So as we went our separate ways professionally, I started to sense the need to find another group of friends, friends who would relate to the path I was on in a way that my old friends were unable to. Some of the directions and risks I was taking were completely new to me, and I needed allies, people who could teach me new skills or perspectives that would make me a better businessman and person. I needed people I loved, like the friends I'd had since my twenties, but also those who could challenge and inspire me.

Friendships hold the potential to contribute to your growth and to your emotional well-being. So it's vital to seek out the company of people you admire, people who are doing big things that you aspire to do. If you are trying to start a business, and all your friends tell you that you're crazy to take a risk, then they're probably not the friends you need. The friends that are worth your time are the ones who will affirm your potential and encourage you to strive toward your most ambitious goals. They are the ones who will be honest with you about the direction they see you headed, even when their opinion is not the one you want to hear.

I am not suggesting you abandon lifelong friends, but understand that others' mindsets, goals, and ambitions affect you. And with that in mind, you should be protective of your time and energy and selective about the people you choose to invest in.

If your current friends are not the best influences, or if you need more people in your circle, try gathering with existing communities of like-minded people. This is a group that is built on deliberately chosen common interests. For example, I am a part of communities with professionals colleagues in real estate and content creation. I am a part of a church community that is there for me through the ups and downs of trying to live by faith and there to celebrate me when I grow or pick me up when I fall. If you don't know where to start, try using Meetup.com, a tool that lets you search for specific interest groups.

The common element in the type of community I am describing is that they are deliberately chosen and cultivated through the collective investment of their members. Communities facilitate an unspoken understanding of the issues that bind their members together. They allow for the exchanging of members' victories and defeats and their hopes and concerns with others who can relate and empathize.

In communities, you can set aside the adversarial and territorial mindset found too often in business and your personal life. Having a group of people that gathers together for growth on a shared path can help remind you that there's a point to what you're doing that extends beyond winning.

The benefits of seeking out communities like those I am describing are rich and multifaceted, offering moral support, advice, feedback, and referrals that grow your network and bolster your accountability. Additionally, joining a community is an ideal way to cultivate positive friendships. There are communities all around you with a great diversity of members, some potential lifelong friends and others who might be your next coach and mentor. But they won't come to you. I suggest you do yourself a favor and seek out and continually invest in the ones that will encourage your journey.

Employees and Coworkers

As I said in the last section, you are the average of the five people you spend the most time with. That's the very reason that workplace relationships are so critical. For most, there will be very few people you spend more time with than the coworkers who share your space for eight hours a day. So, when I look for an employee, attitude is everything.

No matter their position, no matter the level of education, experience, or expertise, an attitude of service to the work community is imperative to their personal success and our success as a company. I am highly choosy when it comes to hiring new employees. I have learned the hard way that just one bad employee can bring down a whole operation. Even one negative attitude can suck the positivity out of a room. To ensure that won't happen, I go so far as to administer personality tests to each prospective employee. I do so because I want to take every precaution necessary to ensure that the person I hire will fit into our company culture, ascribe to our core values, and invest in our shared community goals.

That is why I am so protective of my work culture. It's why I spend so much time and energy on the front end, minimizing the likelihood a toxic person finds their way into my company. It is also why I am quick to fire. If there is a bad apple, I pluck it.

This pertains not just to the people who share your workspace but to the person in the mirror. For better or for worse, your attitude is contagious. And just as one person's bad attitude can drag everyone down, so can the positive attitude of another.

Those with an attitude of generosity of their time and energy toward their colleagues are true Wealth Builders. They are always looking for ways to further the growth of their coworkers and the company. Those are the individuals who can change lives from the company's bottom all the way to the very top.

Social Media Followers

The world of social media can seem like every man for himself. So many make a post and look for what they can get from it. They're starving for likes, comments, shares, and saves. They want acclaim. In the process, they overlook that behind those numbers are real people who, for some reason, have decided to lend their precious time and attention to what you have to say.

Remember the "social" in social media when you post. Take your followers very seriously by considering the content you produce as an opportunity for service and generosity. Go to bat for them. Do whatever you can do, and give whatever you can give to help them succeed through the content that you put out there for them to see.

I would be lying if I claimed that social media has not helped me financially or that I don't notice when my content fails to engage the audience. In truth, it has made me far more money and generated more business than I could have ever imagined. Nevertheless, I believe that the success I have had is paradoxical. Through producing content with the intention of giving away value, social media has given me value back tenfold.

But what I have gotten back from this approach extends far beyond the financial. Some of the most meaningful rewards I have gained from my social media presence are through follower feedback, people who've shared with me the impact I've had in their lives, and the ways that they are thriving as a result of something I posted.

If you are active on social media and disappointed with the impact and reach of your content, I suggest you adopt a giving mindset. Of course, we all like our generosity reciprocated, but your social media presence can't depend on that.

Accept that building a community may take time and investment, just as it does in the "real" world outside of social media. Also, realize that not everyone on social media is social, but just about everyone is on social media. You never know the impact you might be making. Your role is to offer your gift—whether they accept and express their appreciation for it is secondary.

Action Items

The people you choose to surround yourself with affect who you become, and how you invest in them determines whether you reap the unmatched benefits the social connection has on your well-being. Here are some ways to ensure you don't lose out:

1. **Prioritize family time.** There may be no easier part of your team to take for granted than your family. Barring a divorce from your spouse or legal emancipation from your parents and siblings, you're pretty much stuck with them, and they're pretty much stuck with you. Make sure you cultivate a habit that reaffirms the importance of that relationship. Start by choosing one family member to which you could give more of your attention. Think of an act that will be personally meaningful to them and commit to engaging in that behavior consistently. Something as small as a once-a-week phone call can make a huge difference in a relationship that's been residing at the bottom of your priority list.

2. **Ask yourself with each new social media post:** *How am I serving my viewers with this content?* The answer doesn't have to be some Mother Teresa-level charitable act, but it's good to keep your motives at the forefront of your mind. If you are posting for self-serving reasons like attention or likes, check in with yourself about why that is important.

3. **Join a community of like-minded individuals.** The community you join depends on where you wish to grow the most. They may be online or in person. They may be social groups, church communities, professional groups, or whatever other group you can think of. I am a member of several mastermind groups where I gather with peers who offer one another mentoring and help in navigating the problems in their lives. I also offer my mastermind called Wealthy Investor (https://

www.wealthyinvestor.com), which brings together people from across the country who are investing their money toward the common goal of improving their lives and their success in real estate. If none of those meet your needs, you can find online forums and communities on LinkedIn, Facebook, and Meetup.com and search by interest. What's important is that you put yourself out there and find your tribe.

Serving Yourself Through Serving Others

As humans, we are wired for connection. Each individual is a unique collection of strengths and weaknesses, likes and dislikes, and experiences and expertise. Consequently, we aren't meant to go it alone but to serve and depend on one another. We need others, and they need us. It's the people around you who give life meaning.

Service is the lifeblood of your relationships. We ultimately neglect ourselves when we neglect the people on our side, whether our family, friends, employees, coworkers or even our social media followers. Ultimately, it is the investment of your time and presence that provides the lifeblood to those who comprise your team.

I invest in my wife and children through a commitment to the times regularly set aside for them. I treat these times as sacred, turning my attention away from work and from anything else that may distract from them. I invest in my relationship with my parents and sister through their regular involvement in my social and professional life. I am intentional in cultivating my friendships and selective about who I associate with but generous with the time I spend with those I call my friends and associates. The same goes for my coworkers and employees; I choose carefully and give freely. And finally, I consider my social media followers to be a part of my team, individuals whose investment of time and energy I aspire to return in abundance.

I am exceedingly grateful to those who are a part of my team. So, I always try to demonstrate my gratitude through my presence. Relationships make us better, happier, and healthier. They epitomize the getting in the giving. Through serving them, we truly serve ourselves.

CHAPTER 15

Health is the Ultimate Wealth

"There is no greater failure than being rich in money and poor in health. There's no point in having money or success when you don't have the energy to use it for good."

—LEWIS HOWES

The last component of WEALTH is health. Your wealth in every other area of your life will not succeed without the health of your body. Put simply, all of the affluence in the world is worth nothing without health because you won't have the capacity to enjoy it.

Money cannot and will not ever buy your way out of the body you live in. It can't cure low energy, chronic pain, the craving for your next cigarette or drink, or self-consciousness about your appearance. Most importantly, if you're dead, that money certainly isn't doing you any good. With a broken body, you are truly broke.

Your health and vitality are the engines behind your wealth building. Your focus, stamina, mood, and even your intelligence are influenced by your overall physical health. The unfit body simply can't carry as great a mental or physical load as the one provided with nourishing fuel and movement. By accepting poor health, a person volunteers to play the game of life with a handicap. In this chapter, I hope to convince you that sacrificing your health is sacrificing your potential.

Diet

When it comes to diet, a troubling tendency among a significant number of adults is to treat their health haphazardly, allowing themselves indulgences that they know to be self-defeating. The same person who eats that extra slice of pie, for example, or the one who drinks several soft drinks or beers, wouldn't dare put the same in their dog's bowl or their child's plate. They recognize clearly that it would be wrong to offer junk food to an animal or a child, but they somehow manage to completely miss the depravity they show themselves when they allow these things to enter their body.

I am no nutrition expert, but I pay close attention to the foods I put into my body, and when it comes to diets, I have tried them all—Atkins, Keto, carb loading, intermittent fasting, and even the carnivore diet. Ultimately, it comes down to your goals. Need to lose a lot of weight? Well, then, something like keto might work for you. Need to gain a bunch? Well, load up on those carbs. It's up to you to view your health as a priority, educate yourself on the specifics of each diet, and experiment to find out which works best for you. Like everything else we have covered, the key ingredient, regardless of the recipe, is purpose. It's being responsive instead of reactive.

With that in mind, the best diet is the one that you keep. For example, if all your favorite foods include meat, you will probably fail on a vegan diet. More important than the diet you choose is your consistency. Not only will dabbling in a diet lead to discouragement, but it will also render any experimenting with its effectiveness null and void. You can't practice keto during the day, eat an ice cream sundae before bed, and conclude that keto doesn't work when you find that the number of your scale isn't changing.

But you need to consider a couple of obstacles when choosing and trying to stick to a diet. We'll start with the latter since that's the part where most people stumble. The sad fact is that food scientists have outsmarted just about everybody who's not paying attention. They've figured out how to process foods that spike blood sugar, hijack brain chemistry, and produce cravings that overpower willpower.

Besides that, you can find someone who claims just about any food is bad for you depending on what they prefer or what they are trying to sell you. Are you going to find a vegan who argues for the health benefits of meat? I can assure you that you won't. But is there an advocate of the carnivore diet who will argue convincingly and with the backing of equally convincing scientific evidence that meat is good for you? Absolutely.

Part of the problem is that there are no one-size-fits-all diets, just as there is no one-size-fits-all sleep regimen or exercise routine. What makes one person feel great will make another feel like crap.

But as I stated, I've tried them all and have talked to scores of nutritionists over the years. I have determined over the years that it's important to find *your* ideal balance of the three macronutrients: fats, carbohydrates, and proteins. Regardless of the diet's name or how trendy it is, I've settled on the "best" diet being the one with the ratio of the three macronutrients that suits your goals. Do you want to gain weight or lose weight? Do you want to gain muscle or burn fat? The answers to all these questions will determine the "best" diet, not what some self-proclaimed guru tells you.

I will share the method I've used with you because it is simple and has worked for me. My goal is to remain strong and maintain an athletic build. I don't want to be massive. I don't necessarily need to be completely free of body fat. I just want to maintain my fitness. And I've found that the best way to maintain my strength is by ensuring that I eat about a gram of protein per pound of body weight each day. That has kept me at 180 pounds for about the last twelve years. At no time has my weight fluctuated by more than five pounds above or below that weight.

The reason is that I follow a budget, just as I do with my money, just as I do with my time. Those ten pounds represent my margin, and I routinely track it to determine whether changes need to be made. When I see that my weight is nearing that upper allowance, I reduce my intake of carbohydrates. When I know I'm losing too much, I add carbs to my diet. It's as simple as that.

Of course, calories matter. I'm certain any inquiring mind could prove that, generally speaking, more calories lead to more weight gain and fewer lead to weight loss. Take my word for it or experiment for yourself, and you'll discover not all calories are created equally. Try eating 2,500 calories composed strictly of protein for a couple of weeks, then switch to 2,500 calories of pure pasta and see if the results are the same. I think you'll find that the quality of your food is just as important if not more than the quantity. But what's most important is that you experiment to determine what works for your body, what you can sustain, and then stick to your budget.

Fasting

There's a reason the Bible talks so much about fasting. In fact, you'd be hard-pressed to find a world religion that does not proclaim the value of abstaining from food or drink for a time. Go ahead—try to find one. Why? Because fasting provides cleansing of body and mind alike, opening a person to receive nourishment in a way that was not possible through their habitual ways of being.

During a fast, the body goes from dependence on food in the form of glucose for energy to reliance on fat stored in the body, a process called ketosis.[40] Detoxification is a fortunate by-product of this process since much of the waste that we build up over time is stored in fat.

This cleansing of toxins is accompanied by a process known as autophagy, the body's way of sending damaged cells packing to clear the path for new, healthy ones to enter the fray.[41] The word *autophagy* comes from a Latin word meaning "self-eating," which points to what happens to faulty cells during a fast—the body breaks them down and uses the leftover raw materials to build new ones.

It's like the body's form of repentance, a term that too often comes with the baggage it's intended to relieve. The excess fat, the toxins, and the old, damaged cells that result from unbridled eating are like the shame, weariness, and discontent of the vices that keep you stuck. But in turning from habitual ways of being that no longer serve our best interests, we open the space to recognize a new way—a better way. For Christians, this "better way" is the renewal of the spirit through Jesus. For the person who forgoes food for a time, the better way comes with a host of benefits—slowed aging, a healthier brain, reduced likelihood of health conditions from Alzheimer's to heart disease to cancer, and the list goes on.[42]

But the shifts resulting from stepping away from our eating habits don't end with the body. They are mirrored by changes in the mind and spirit. Fasting is the antidote to gluttony and entitlement. With ready and unconditional access to food comes a certain arrogant and

---

40 Seliger, Susan. "Is Fasting Healthy." WebMD. February 23, 2007. https://www.webmd.com/diet/features/is_fasting_healthy.

41 Lindberg, Sara. "Autophagy: What You Need to Know." Healthline. August 23, 2018. https://www.healthline.com/health/autophagy.

42 Rachael Link, "8 Health Benefits of Fasting, Backed by Sciences," Healthline, July 30, 2018, https://www.healthline.com/nutrition/fasting-benefits.

blissful ignorance of the possibility that things could be any other way. But by declining the invitation to escape hunger, the impulse that declares it time for a trip to the fridge, a person retakes the reins from the whims of appetite. They voluntarily toss aside the crutch of unconditional access to food to encounter their own vulnerability. In doing so, they also have vivid hindsight on how much they took for granted the privilege of always having food readily at their service.

Just as the body turns from dependence on external sources of sustenance to internal sources, the mind and spirit turn inward for relief when no outside sources are available. I recently discovered this when I abstained from food over a five-day period.

There are numerous stories in the Bible of individuals fasting to humble their spirits so they may rely more fully on God for strength and guidance. In fact, Jesus himself, as noted in Matthew 4:1-11, fasted for forty days and nights in preparation for his three-year ministry—one that would go on to define his life. So when I recently found myself lost in the direction God wanted me to go, I decided to begin a five-day fast of my own, three more than I had done up to that point.

In the days that followed, there were certainly times that I struggled, times my body cried out for relief from headaches, fatigue, lightheadedness, and of course, hunger. But during those times I normally would have eaten, I turned to Jesus through prayer and scripture reading. When all was said and done, I had lost ten pounds and felt physically and mentally sharper than ever. But this paled in comparison to the benefits I reaped in my spiritual health. I felt closer to Jesus, more grateful and grounded. Like the toxins and the cells that no doubt underwent a transformation in my body, my spirit felt cleansed and renewed.

So maybe you're now considering a fast of your own. But you have a lot to do, and you might be concerned that fasting will handicap your ability to function, think clearly, and act energetically. If that's the case, you may be surprised to find out the recent discovery that fasting actually *increases* the ability to concentrate.[43] Not only that, but you might be surprised to discover that abstaining from food for a time offers one of the most potent accelerants to the production of growth hormone, which promotes muscle growth and energy levels.[44] If that's not enough to convince you, then consider also the increase in adrenaline that occurs as a result of fasting. The result is that you feel more awake and alert as your body turns to fat for fuel. Researchers have surmised that these changes might relate to our long history of imposed fasting; because we couldn't always run down to Whole Foods to grab our meat, fruits and berries, we needed to be alert and full of energy *especially* when no food was available.

Make no mistake, you may moan and groan for relief like I sometimes did during my recent fast. Particularly in industrialized countries like America, a significant proportion of the population is used to waving their hands like a young king at the first sign of hunger or boredom, knowing food will then appear on their plate like magic. When this isn't allowed, hunger pangs are the natural result. But these feelings pass, and the body and spirit will compensate in all the miraculous ways I have covered to this point.

So all that's left is choosing the form your particular fast will take, and there are many to choose from:

- The 5:2 diet, where a person eats for five days and fasts for two

- Alternate-day fasting, which is just as it sounds, one day on, one day off.

---

43 Kean, Nikki. "Study Dispels Myths on Intermittent Fasting for Weight Loss" Clinical Advisor. April 5, 2022. https://www.clinicaladvisor.com/home/topics/diet-and-nutrition-information-center/study-dispels-myths-intermittent-fasting/.

44 Catenacci et al. "A randomized pilot study comparing zero-calorie alternate-day fasting to daily caloric restriction in adults with obesity." Obesity 24, no. 9 (2016): 1874-1883.

- Time-restricted eating, where an individual eats during a given window of time, usually four to twelve hours, and fasts for the remainder of the twenty-four hours

- Prolonged fasts like the one I did, when I replaced the time I would normally spend eating with seeking direction from God.

The right one is the one that works for you, and, in fact, all have been found to produce similar outcomes.[45] So I urge you to choose one because, through fasting, you'll gain a greater appreciation for what you have and what your mind, body, and spirit are capable of. And with that knowledge, you will face struggle with a renewed sense of strength and grace when it arrives uninvited.

Exercise

Along with its obvious benefits to your physical health and appearance, exercise affects your mental acuity. It affects your productivity. Certainly, I can say this from experience, but it's not just conjecture. There is enough evidence for the benefits of exercise to your mental health that you simply cannot claim to be your best without it. If you neglect your body, then you are doing yourself a disservice and falling short of your full potential.

This is going to sound very familiar. Working in a profession that depended largely on the fitness of my body, I have probably had experience with more workouts than 99 percent of the population—high reps and low reps, workouts with high intensity and short duration, workouts with moderate intensity and long duration, Crossfit, hot

---

45 Jason Fung, *"The Obesity Code"* (Vancouver/Berkeley: Greystone Books, 2016).

yoga, cold yoga. Well, maybe not that last one, but the point is I have done a lot of experimenting when it comes to workouts.

One thing I haven't experienced is a workout that doesn't produce results. If your body is moving, then your body is working. So, my advice remains as straightforward for exercise as it is for diet. Step one, pick something. Step two, do it consistently. If you can't be consistent, you can't expect consistent results, so switch to something you won't flake out on.

Get creative. You can find some kind of physical activity you enjoy. At worst, you can settle on something you prefer to the other alternatives. Some people love to run, and it doesn't take a genius to know that they are more likely to stick with a running routine than those who would only choose to run if they were being chased. But don't force yourself to endure something that makes you utterly miserable because it's unnecessary. I maintain my fitness despite being far from a running connoisseur. I don't enjoy running, so I rarely do it because there are limitless options for workouts.

Granted, there are unique benefits to cardiovascular work and resistance training that you can't get from the other—the mirror will likely tell a different story for the person who commits to a year of running versus the one who lifts weights for a year. The point is that many options exist for building a physically fit body. You can get elite cardiovascular health through running, swimming, or biking, just as sure as you can get it through martial arts, climbing, or dancing. You can build strength through weight training, bodyweight exercises like CrossFit, and certain types of yoga.

Along with deciding the kind of workout that is best for you, you have to decide the time of day and frequency that you'll do it. But what's best? Again, put the question aside because there are as many arguments for morning versus night workouts as vegan versus omnivore diets. The fact is, there are so many viewpoints and variables that you might as well let one override all of the others: your preference.

Although the time that you work out is not all that crucial, it would be hard to make the same argument for how much you work out. Obviously, you will get next to nothing from working out once a month, just as you'll get next to nothing from exercising one minute a day. There's also undoubtedly such a thing as overtraining. A body that is given no time to rest and recover also has no time to rebuild and grow to accommodate the demands being put on it. Work out for three hours a day, seven days a week, and the likely outcomes are injury and even *decreased* performance. Work out for twelve hours in one day, and, well, I suggest keeping the hospital on speed dial.

If you have decided it's time to begin a consistent routine, start small and expect that there will be some struggle; getting a boulder moving from a standstill is the hardest part. If you haven't been to a gym in years, then setting out to lift weights two hours a day, five times a week, is setting yourself up for discouragement and frustration. Working out too much too fast is destined to fail because your body is not used to it, and your mind will fight you. Seek small victories and remember what the R in SMART goals stands for: what's ideal might not be what's realistic.

I've found it helps tremendously to rope in a workout partner to come with you or, better yet, a coach. Both have advantages, but either will bring some extra accountability to your intention and make it much more likely that you will follow through. And remember: the best workout is the one you're going to do.

Personally, I have found two workouts a week for about an hour each to be the bare minimum just to maintain my current level of health. Any less than that, I notice a decline in my fitness and performance. On the other hand, five workouts are the most I can perform without experiencing diminishing returns or even a little backsliding. Ideally, I lift weights four times a week.

Hobbies for Health

For some, the thought of running aimlessly for half an hour or picking up and putting down iron objects repeatedly until your body gives out sounds like torture. But what if you found hobbies that worked your body and didn't *feel* like work? The point is to stay active; misery is not a prerequisite to fitness.

I'm not suggesting you give up the more traditional types of exercise if they're a bit uncomfortable initially. I doubt I loved lifting weights the first time I got underneath a barbell, but eventually, I came to crave it. But I do encourage you to find an active hobby. Sports, for example, provide a great alternative (or addition) to the activities we typically associate with working out, and as a person who loves sports and competition, I have scores of fond memories of feeling utterly exhausted after a game, both mentally and physically, despite never having set out to "work out."

It doesn't matter your age. It doesn't matter your current level of fitness. Choosing to take up a sport doesn't mean you have to aspire to become a professional, but you may well pick up a passion that has the side effect of keeping you healthy and sharp. For example, I play golf and basketball regularly, and I can tell you from experience that it is often as exhausting as fun.

In addition to the physical benefits of sports, competition is a great driver of motivation. It will bring out the best of you and push your will farther than you could have imagined. If you're trying to win (or not to lose), you're going to use every calorie at your disposal to make it happen.

Action Items

Do you want to feel better, look hotter, sleep deeper, live longer, and get more done? Probably. But if you aren't paying attention to eating right and working out, you're trading all of these benefits for a few moments of empty pleasure and relief that inevitably lead to long-term suffering. Here are a few suggestions that may help move you toward a healthier and better you:

1. **Leverage the power of stimulus control.** Do you know what the strongest predictor of self-control failure is? Hint: it has more to do with your environment than with you. Self-control failure is most likely when temptations are closest. Isn't it obvious that the ice cream in that bowl on your lap will be harder to resist than the one still in the refrigerator? And isn't it just as obvious that you'll be less likely to drive to the store to satisfy your craving than walking over to your freezer? Take advantage of this principle when it comes to dieting and working out. Shop on a full belly and buy only the things you want to have at your disposal. Lay out your workout clothes the night before, so one less thing stands in the way of you getting your body in motion.

2. **Journal your way to motivation.** Knowing that you "probably should" work out is not a recipe for motivation to work out or satisfaction when you do. Getting clear on your purpose, though, will accomplish both. Spending about thirty minutes or so writing the answers to these questions: What do I want to get out of this? What is preventing me from doing it? How will other areas of my life look if I improve my health?

3. **Now get moving.** The CDC recommends you exercise at least three times a week for a minimum of twenty minutes. That's it—twenty minutes. You're lying to yourself if you claim you don't have twenty minutes. Get off the couch and do something,

anything. If you're accustomed to doing nothing, then a regular walk will pay huge dividends relative to the small investment of time and energy you make in your physical and mental health.

Persistent Practice, Persistent Pleasure

The cruel irony is that healthy living doesn't seem to come naturally but requires planning and discipline. It seems we're wired to self-sabotage, and our environments are happy to oblige. When you get home, and you're hungry, the easiest thing to do and the quickest path to pleasure is to reach for the pack of Oreos sitting on the top shelf of your pantry. When you're tired, the quickest path to relief is to plop down, glaze over, and tune out. But think about it. How do you feel once that's over? And what's that accomplishing for you? Is what you're choosing expanding your well-being or your waistline?

I urge you to consider the alternative. When you walk in the door after a long day of work, and you're so hungry that it feels like you've skipped the past five meals, remind yourself this: the healthy option isn't the easiest, but it will provide pleasure that lasts long beyond a sugar rush. When you feel too tired to do anything but lay on the couch and watch Netflix, remember that going out and getting some exercise isn't the easiest thing to do, but it will provide greater relief from what ails you than an hour of vegging ever will. The best healthy lifestyle is the one you follow- set yourself up for success by establishing diet and exercise habits that work for you for good.

CHAPTER 16

Who Says You Can't Get Rich Quick?

"The single biggest financial mistake I've made was not thinking big enough. I encourage you to go for more than a million. There is no shortage of money on this planet, only a shortage of people thinking big enough."

— GRANT CARDONE

I got into real estate investing eight years ago. All that was in my wallet at the time was a few bucks and a handful of maxed out credit cards that had allowed me to kick down the door to this industry. If I had walked into Dave Ramsey's office back then, I suspect he would have snatched my wallet away and cut up my credit cards himself, but he would've missed the point. And I would've missed out on the ride of my life.

This wasn't a haphazard decision. One thing I was sure of was that I could find and close deals. I belonged in this industry, and I was willing to bet everything on that. In fact, I bet more than everything. I maxed those credit cards out by necessity, because I didn't have the money to buy and flip a house. If I failed, I wouldn't be at square one—I'd be at square -50,000. But I knew that money was the only thing standing in my way. If I could just find one, I truly believed that this industry would be mine for the taking.

At the time, everyone was singing the same tune. *Flipping's a one-and-done deal, don't waste your time with that. Passive income is the name of the game—you gotta start buying rentals.* I was hearing all this and thinking, "Dude, this doesn't make sense. Why would I hang on to a property that's going to make me 200 bucks a month when I could flip one and walk away with twenty grand in my pocket that I could use to buy another one?" Once I did that, I figured I could buy two more—rinse and repeat. In other words, my colleagues saw a fool-proof route to slow and steady money. But I saw the on-ramp to an expressway where I could get rich at breakneck speed.

People are still buying into the ol' tortoise-and-hare myth. *Buy a rental here, another one there, and just keep saving up every year.* No! Figure out how to make $250,000, and live on very little of it. From there, begin to hire and delegate—turn that 250,000 into a million doing the same thing, only better. By then you'll be off to the races, investing that money to branch off into new spheres of influence, finding ways to make money from your money. It's through scaling that people make the kind of money that changes the trajectory of their lives and expands the reach of their influence. A rental property that gets you a few hundred bucks a month isn't going to do that. In this story, the hare passes the tortoise and never looks back.

I wasn't interested in a slow, leisurely stroll. Thankfully, this turned out to be a case where my unapologetic, single-minded ambition—or what the tortoises of the world might call impatience and stubbornness—worked in my favor. I didn't buy rentals at all during my first three years in the business. And once I reached a million through house flipping, I was so heavily focused on reinvesting every dollar—into my deals and my people—that rentals remained an afterthought. Just as I had calculated when I decided to ignore the so-called voices of reason and drive straight into the expressway's teeth, flipping had turned out to be a capital-intensive ride, and the proof was in the pudding.

It wasn't until 2018, three years into the real estate game and well past a million dollars in revenue from my bread and butter, that I really started buying some rentals. I began with a ten-unit apartment in Las Vegas. Over the next three years, I earned a slow, steady, and passive income, just as my friends had contended. But that wasn't the point. In 2022, the ten-unit apartment building I picked up for $300,000 sold for $1.2 million. During that time I bought up Airbnbs in Big Bear and have watched those appreciate by over $2 million dollars since.

Rentals weren't the only new venture I began in 2018. I also started the groundwork for what would become Forever Home Realty, my real estate brokerage, which I owned and operated for almost five years. After that, I began Future Flipper (now rebranded to Wealthy Investor), my first education company and the beginning of a phase of giving back that continues with this book and the Wealthy Way movement that preceded it. And I wasn't done. A year later, I started TrueBooks, a company aimed at helping investors and entrepreneurs pay less tax. It's the kind of CPA firm I wish I'd had access to when I was starting out. You get the picture. I was doubling and tripling down on the capital I'd saved through my foundational skill, investing it in ways that would multiply my reach and my earning potential.

This time, just as before, my colleagues had plenty to say about the sensibility of my plan, "No, dude, no. Just go buy assets!" In other words, they were continuing with the same logic of taking the path of least resistance to securing passive income. Granted, many of them took that path and are doing fine today. In fact, any American will recognize the logic: go to work, do your job, build on your 401(k) for retirement. For me, that's the equivalent of waiting for something I could take in a couple of years and build an empire from.

Listen, if you want to take the Dave Ramsey approach, keep your head down, live below your means, and have a W-2 your whole life, fine. Maybe you'll be one of the few who manages to reach a million bucks in twenty years, and more power to you. I'm not here to hate on anyone.

Nevertheless, that's the long, slow path of restraint, delay, and "stability." Usually, it requires you to deny yourself a lot today, where life happens, in anticipation of the life you'll live to the fullest when, God willing, you get there.

But since you've read to the end of this book, I'm going to assume you want more for your life than that. You don't want to bide your time and wait for wealth to come to you. You want to go and take it. And that's where this framework comes in. Come on. Let me show you how to get rich as quickly as I did.

Get Rich Quick: Make-Manage-Multiply

Getting rich quick has a bad reputation. But why? Is there any person who can say with a straight face that they'd prefer to wait on abundance when another route exists that would get them there in a fraction of the time? Naysayers will insist no route exists, but naysaying is the language of the hater.

"I had to walk fifteen miles to school, barefoot and with snow up to my thighs," they say.

"Well I'm sorry to hear that, sir. I guess it's a good thing we now have snowplows, salt for the roads, and a bus system ... but why weren't you wearing shoes?" The young, ambitious men and women I talk to today aren't interested in whether or not getting rich quickly has a good or bad reputation—they want it, and they believe it's possible to achieve. They already possess the most important ingredient to fast track to wealth: belief. But I want to give them something I didn't have when I ventured out into the virtual unknown: a road map. Luckily I drew one up as I went, a proven framework I call 3M: *Make-Manage-Multiply*.

What does it really take to build wealth? For me, the answer grew out of a years-long process of trial and error and self-discovery. Of course, living the Wealthy Way provides the foundation. But what else?

I've recently set out to formalize the business side of the Wealthy Way. Just as I tackled lifestyle in the pages leading up to this chapter, I sought to get clear on what I believe constitutes true success in business. What are the steps to achieving success? And what constitutes "success" anyway? Is it passive income? Becoming a millionaire? Of course, the answers to these questions and the bounds of personal ambition will vary from person to person. Nevertheless, I want to offer you my vision of business success, both the road and the destination. And my goal is clarity: a series of steps that will put you, the reader, in the driver's seat to your version of success in business.

There is a simple formula that applies no matter where you are in the process of building the business of your dreams. But the first part of that process is determining what stage you're in—after all, a map is useless if you don't know your starting point. We break the process into three M's: Make, Manage, and Multiply. Let's look at these stages one by one.

Stage One: Make

If you're this far into this book, you already understand the importance of developing a core moneymaking skill. Do you possess one skill that, if fully developed and leveraged, could make you $250,000 in a year on its own? That's your moneymaker. And there's no way around it—the fast track starts in the trenches. You have to identify that skill and commit to investing the majority of your time, energy, and money—even if it comes from a stack of maxed-out credit cards—to developing it and putting it to work toward building capital. Sure, it's good to be well-rounded, but make this one skill your foundation and your priority. Don't get bogged down in everything else—make it your mission to sharpen your best tools.

I see too many people who are putting in their hours, working toward their realtors license, creating a little social media content here and there, or trying out a side hustle "when they have time." They have all these half-commitments they're dabbling in. Then a couple of years go by, and they're still working the same job they hoped to leave if one of those half-baked attempts caught on.

Tim Ferriss was right when he said, "What you don't do determines what you can do." Momentum comes from effort continuously applied in a single direction, and constantly shifting gears is a surefire formula for stifling momentum. It's only by putting 99 percent more time and commitment into our core skill that we become a one-percenter in that area. And you have to possess elite skills to earn an elite income. If every average Joe or Jane were good enough for a quarter-million dollars a year, half the population would be making a quarter-million dollars a year. So first, choose. What's your thing?

As you'll recall, I was a crap realtor. My job was to sell what already was and perhaps make the case for what it could be. In other words, I could lead a horse to water, but I couldn't force it to drink. I had a knack for finding a good deal, but making any money from my ability to find a diamond in the rough depended on the buyer's ability to recognize a diamond when they saw one, too.

With the money I borrowed from credit card companies, I could finally find, buy, and polish the diamonds that others failed to recognize. With the money from those, I could buy more and better ones. By the end of my second year of house flipping I surpassed the $250,000 mark and earned my passage from Stage One to Stage Two.

My results and my competence testified that, if necessary, this was a skill I could bank on exclusively and indefinitely. If I did nothing else, I could earn a solid living on house flipping alone. I do believe that house flipping is one of the most reliable ways to get to this solid living, but it is not the only way. I have plenty of buddies and colleagues who create content and earn more than $250,000 through ad revenue and sponsorships alone. I know others who have leveraged their skills in digital marketing to earn a high salary through affiliate marketing, funneling customers toward products like mine. In fact, I've managed to earn six figures per year promoting others' products despite this task comprising a very small portion of my time and effort. I didn't have to create it, I didn't have to build a brand for it, I didn't have to fulfill it—-I simply promoted businesses that I believed in enough to put my name behind them.

Another option is to start a more traditional business, making your money from a product or service that you can uniquely deliver. I'm amazed at the popularity couch flipping has gained since I first made a YouTube video about it, but I'm unsurprised by the testimonials of those who have proven it possible to make $250,000 doing it. There are plenty who have earned a quarter million dollars selling their products online—clothing, artwork, services like programming or copywriting—the possibilities are endless. If you can sell a million dollars of product at 25 percent margin for a net $250,000, then great—you just cleared Stage One in the game of business.

So, by all means pick a skill that suits you, but I can attest that real estate offers one of the most direct and reliable vehicles to $250,000, and I've created a program called the Wealthy Investor (wealthyinvestor.com) to help you navigate your way there. I recommend real estate for a few reasons. One, you have many options through which $250,000 is a feasible goal. You can flip ten modest houses at twenty five grand a pop or five high-end houses at fifty thousand each. There's your 250. You could wholesale. Again, let's say your wholesale fee is $10,000. Wholesale twenty five homes—two a month—and you're there. And there's a third way: Airbnb. It's absolutely possible to gross a million bucks and net 250 through Airbnb. How do I know that's possible? Because I've seen it done, and I created a program through the Wealthy Investor called ProHost that offers the ins and outs of maximizing profits through Airbnb.

But the reason I prefer real estate to all the side hustles I have tried is that it provides limitless opportunities to those willing to continually hone their skills. And the skills you build during this moneymaking stage of your business development will readily translate to your success in Stages Two and Three. Real estate involves negotiation, sales, and marketing operations—many of the skills that prepare you for success in other businesses.

If you stay focused on honing your core moneymaking skill in Stage One, the results will follow, and your first year of $250,000+ will represent your rite of passage to Stage Two. You will waste your time by trying to jump ahead if you're not there yet. Why? Because you need to become an expert at one thing first. There is no rule against trying other things. Maybe you try real estate and decide it is not for you. There is no rule against cutting your losses and trying something else. You can always come back to it.

That's what happened to me. I returned to real estate when I realized that it wasn't the game I didn't like, it was that I was playing the wrong position. I was an investor and a deal-maker, not an agent. But don't "try on" real estate for a month and conclude, "Well, that didn't work." Of course it didn't! Lackluster efforts produce lackluster results.

For the same reason, avoid trying too many things at once, hoping one will stick out as the clear favorite. By all means, brainstorm all possible avenues to $250,000, but remember: none will get you there until you pick and persist with one. In Stage One, you are setting the roots from which your business will grow. Your daily efforts at this stage will serve as the foundation of everything that is to come.

Stage Two: Manage

Once you've established this foundation and earned $250,000 in a year, you can move on to Stage Two: Manage. This is the stage at which your earning potential and reach are limited by your individual capacity to keep up. In other words, the demand for your core moneymaking skill outpaces your ability to supply it. So, how do you continue to grow your business? By scaling.

Stage Two contains two critical elements. The first is hiring and managing people. Here, it is essential that ample time is invested into vetting your potential employees. Of course, you want to hire those who are skilled in the job functions you intend to pass on, but it is ultimately the character of the people you hire that will determine whether they prove to be an asset or a liability. Simply put, individuals with integrity and initiative will be the easiest to manage and require the least oversight. This brings us to the second element of Stage Two: removing yourself from day-to-day operations.

Assuming you've taken the time to hire and fully train the right people, you can cut back on the low-value aspects of your work and focus your time and efforts on exercising high-value tasks. You can redirect the time you'd normally spend carrying out the tasks now assigned to your employees to family, hobbies, travel—whatever you choose is the best investment of your time. Remember, the Wealthy Way is about lifestyle. This is where you build the margin in your time to bring intention to designing the life you want to live.

Scale your business and free up your time by hiring some people to do the work. Sounds easy, right? In truth, hiring people and building the kind of businesses that can run without you requires skill. It's not easy. But you've figured out how to leverage your core skill into

$250,000. Now the goal is to leverage that skill to a million dollars net, this time as a boss, letting other people make the money for you.

Does that mean you'll completely withdraw from the business? Not likely. But if you've been acting as deal-maker and project manager in your house-flipping business, for example, you might be able to delegate the management side to someone else and use the time you free up to find deals that pay more than what it costs to hire someone to manage your projects. You'll also be relieved of a part of the job you don't like and aren't good at. Are you spending a significant portion of your work day on low-paying administrative tasks, like paperwork and emails, that could be delegated for much less than the value of your core skills? It's time to delegate.

Hiring and scaling your business during Stage Two buys you two things: revenue and time. But there's an important point to consider here—just because your revenue goes up doesn't mean your net income will follow. Hiring salespeople, marketers, and administrative assistants costs money, and spending money reduces your margin. Many discover at Stage Two that business revenue is going through the roof, but they're bringing home less money.

Seems obvious, right? Well, it's something that many entrepreneurs overlook. "I was making more money when I was doing it all on my own!" Well of course, but there's a cap on what you can do on your own. You might be able to make half a million bucks working on your own, but generally speaking, the seven-figure salaries are reserved for those who have assembled a team to execute their vision.

Let's say you begin to hire and scale, and your net stays the same. That's still a win when it's accomplished through sharing the work and freeing up your time, right? I don't know about you, but making the same money for less hours represents a massive win for me. In fact, it's the sole measure I use to determine my success in business— not by gross profit or even net profit, but by the increase in my hourly income. In other words, how valuable is my time? Because who do you think enjoys the better quality of life, the person putting in four hours a week to bring in $500,000 or the one working forty-plus hours to make $700,000. The second person has more money, but who has more room to grow? The one who works less.

Now let's say you've done all this and earned the luxury of taking for granted that the people you've trained and the systems you've put into place will run without a hitch while you spend your time on the tasks that produce the greatest results. Business is booming, and your earnings have surpassed the million dollar mark. It's time to move on to Stage Three.

Stage Three: Multiply

So, you've hired some good employees, managed them well enough to take a step back, and netted a cool mill'. This million dollars can be accumulated over a couple of years, it doesn't have to all be in one. Ideally, though, we want to build a business that can net a million yearly at some point. Once you've accomplished all of this, you're ready to move onto Stage Three: Multiply.

Investing is the name of the game at this level. While growth in revenue was largely the product of your time and skills in Stages One and Two, Stage Three is about using money to make money. With your available capital, you can invest into your current business and take it from a seven-figure business to eight figures and beyond. You can branch off into new business ventures, as I did in 2018 when I started Forever Home Realty. Buying stocks is another viable option, so long as it aligns with your expertise or follows the advice of experts in that particular market. And of course, you can continue to invest in real estate, which I opted to do when I expanded my reach to Airbnbs and apartment complexes.

So, how do you know when it's time to move on to Stage Three, aside from the extra zero in your earnings statement? Your business has taken on a life of its own. It's firing on all cylinders with minimal oversight, growing without further investment, and providing a large margin of spending beyond your cost of living. As I mentioned, it wasn't until this stage that I began to shift my focus to anything besides my house-flipping business. I had my team in place and all were on the same page—we could do this in our sleep. But I wasn't interested in sleeping, and I could see that I now had the money, the assets, and the bandwidth to expand our reach far wider than it had been to that point. It was time to multiply.

And that brings me to my present—Stage Three. I'm multiplying, continuing to keep my eye toward the horizon, and using my money and skills to grow my businesses and improve the lives of my team and my audience. When I started out, real estate was my most valuable asset. Today, my priority has shifted to my businesses. Every day I'm working to grow and improve the businesses that I built from the bottom up. And guess what? The day will probably come when I sell them the same way I sold houses in the beginning. Because, like the homes I bought and flipped, I've put the work and systems in place that ensure that the businesses I sell will be worth significantly more value than when I acquired them.

As I've made clear, I know of no stronger foundation than real estate, but it's no accident that the richest people in the world own businesses. Real estate offers a reliable, but grueling, path to wealth. Owning businesses puts you on the fast track.

Why Wait?

Think back on where you were eight years ago. My guess is that it doesn't seem that long ago. Well, in that time I've gone from a broker-than-broke unknown to the owner of seven seven-to-eight-figure businesses with two million followers on social media. Needless to say, it's been a whirlwind, but none of this happened by accident. I didn't get rich quick because I hit the lotto or jumped on the crypto bandwagon when it first got rolling.

No, I got rich by committing to a core moneymaking skill from which I could build the next five years of my business life. I got rich quick by ignoring advice to follow the gradual, reliable path to mediocrity. I can promise you that if I had gone the route encouraged by many of my friends at the time—buying a rental property or two, bringing in a regular but modest stream of passive income, and waiting until it made sense to resell—I would not be where I am today. Bide your time at the outset, and more than likely you'll be biding your time forever—the first step is to build a deep well of capital to pull from, not the last.

I realized that I needed to make a lot of money actively and from the outset in order to live an extraordinary lifestyle and to make extraordinary investments, the kinds that multiply exponentially. I realized I had to focus on one thing, and so I focused on becoming the best house flipper I could be—Stage One. Then I learned how to hire and manage people, to balance the importance of providing a good living for my employees with the importance of continuing my own financial growth. I also began to understand what's necessary to grow a business that operates without active oversight and management—Stage Two. And finally, I learned to reinvest the money in ways that expanded my net worth and my reach. I redoubled investment in my team. I built out my studio and invested in state-of-the-art camera equipment that would allow me to produce social media content that stood out from the crowd. I found ways to use the money I'd earned to venture out in new directions and offer new services—Stage Three.

Just remember, there's more to life than business and financial abundance. It is entirely possible that you could get rich following the Make-Manage-Multiply framework and go broke by neglecting your health, faith, family, and everything else. Don't bother—it's not worth it. But if you can progress through these stages and grow your businesses in a way that frees you up to invest further in the things that lead to true wealth—well, take it from someone who's walked that path, it's a beautiful thing. That's the life of purpose and fulfillment, the life of true wealth.

Want to make a mountain of money quick? There's no shame in that. But the conventional routes of saving and investing in IRAs—even the trendy path of investing in rental properties—won't get you there. But the steps I've shared with you will.

Don't let anyone deter you. Go for it.

Conclusion

When people reach the end of their days and their highlight reel flashes through their minds, what do they remember? Maybe they see that magical evening they spent with their spouse where they kayaked down the river to a secret bank, opened a bottle of wine as the sun descended beneath the horizon, and cried together, talking about their love for their children. Maybe they remember the thing their father said to them before he passed or the radiant look on their child's face when she finished the piano recital she'd practiced so hard for. Maybe it's when they felt God's presence from the top of a mountain or the edge of the sea.

Or do they remember their long hours at the office and all of the money they made? Do they remember the richness of their bank account or the richness of the moments of their lives? Who's there to wipe their tears away, the people that love them or the stack of printed paper at their bedside?

People say time is money, but how depressing is that? Who in their last moments says, "My time was money," without a tinge of regret? Time is not money. No, money is time. The value of time far exceeds money. Money is as good as useless if you're not investing it toward the richness of your time. In fact, it may be worse than useless. For those whose tight grip on money blinded them to time and experience passing them by, money was the thief of life.

Many self-proclaimed experts and gurus offer blueprints to financial wealth without hinting that there's anything more to life. There are the "hustlers" who romanticize using every hour of life, including those rightfully meant for sleep, to grow their status and bank account. And some endorse postponing living until you've saved enough money to earn the right to strive for something more.

I hope that I have offered you another way, one that will change your life for the better. I hope that what you have taken from these pages will lead you to a life of abundance that permeates every area of your life.

It comes down to growing your wealth in each area of life through applying the aspects of the Wealth Builder mindset that were covered in part one- willingness to take risks for the sake of growth, exercising discipline, embodying a spirit of generosity, and humbly committing to your own path and purpose. It's about treating your time as the precious resource that it is, the one whose worth is realized in its entirety when there is none left to spend. It's quiet enough to hear the Spirit so that when that time comes, you can rest knowing you assented to its invitations to the life of your dreams. And it comes down to being consistently responsible for caring for the gifts entrusted to us: our mind, body, and spirit, our family, friends, coworkers, and, yes, our money and belongings.

Action Items

I hope what you read here has helped you and that we can continue our relationship. Below are some ways you can join the ever-growing community of Wealth Builders and bring the Wealthy Way into the world.

1. **Share this with the people on your team: your family, friends, coworkers, and followers.** I hope this book will change the world, and you can help me make that happen and help someone you care about in the process. Whether you share yours or

buy another, offer someone you care about to become a Wealth Builder themselves.

2. **Join the Wealthy Way community at wealthyway.com.** Here, you will have access to a host of resources to continue your journey, including free courses, groups, blogs, the planner, and more.

3. **Begin the Wealthy Way 60.** Research suggests that it takes about sixty days to form a new habit.[46] The Wealthy Way 60 is a great way to try something new and see where it takes you. I challenge you to commit to the following for sixty days:

   - Pray or meditate for ten minutes.

   - Read for twenty minutes.

   - Work on a new stream of income for thirty minutes.

   - Talk with someone for fifteen minutes to see how they're doing.

   - Exercise for forty-five minutes and stick to a diet.

These tasks add up to two hours each day, and those who have followed through on the challenge have reaped remarkable benefits.

Sooner Than You Think

Remember, time is your most valuable resource. Invest wisely in it, producing wealth far beyond the financial. Becoming a Wealth Builder doesn't happen overnight, but putting these habits into practice will soon become second nature, and the results will be worth it—and it may happen sooner than you think.

---

46 Phillippa Lally, Cornelia HM Van Jaarsveld, Henry WW Potts, and Jane Wardle. "How are habits formed: Modelling habit formation in the real world." *European journal of social psychology* 40, no. 6 (2010): 998-1009.

If you'd like to book a free consultation with my team to see how we can help you, scan the QR code below.

Join the Wealthy Way

We provide all the programs and tools you
need to start building wealth today.

Are you interested in building wealth through
real estate investing? *We can help.*
Are you interested in building wealth
through creating content? *We can help.*
Are you interested in building wealth through
growing a business? *We can help.*

Our community of Wealth Builders is strong across the
world. We have students who have been able to quit
their jobs and go full time into entrepreneurship and
investing. We also have students who have been able to
scale and become millionaires. I would love to help you
reach the next stage of your career in building wealth!

If that sounds good to you, please follow the link
below to *book a free strategy call with my team* to
find out how we can help you reach the next level.

↓

WEALTHYWAY.COM

Acknowledgments

The Wealthy Way would not exist without all of the amazing people in my life. I'm thankful to have family, friends, mentors, and employees who have supported me all these years. Without them I would not have been able to accomplish a fraction of the things I share in this book.

I have to give a special thank you to my wife Mindy who has been integral in helping me see the big picture of life beyond just business. She has supported me through every crazy idea and has always helped me believe that anything is possible. On top of that her ability to be an amazing mother to James and Olivia is something I'm so grateful for.

Thank you to the team at Fresh Complaint for helping me bring this dream to life: Zack Williamson for your help in research and writing, Denise McGrail and Ashton Renshaw for your editing genius, and Kelsey Baldwin for designing the interior and cover. And special thanks to Jeff Goins and Chantel Hamilton for your leadership and vision. I couldn't have done it without you!

Lastly but most importantly, I have to give praise to my Lord and savior Jesus Christ. My faith in God is what guides me everyday in a world that is so unpredictable. All of the best decisions I've made have been from obediently following the Holy Spirit. I believe that His fingerprints are all over this book and I'm excited to see how many lives it changes.

I hope that your life is one of them.

About The Author

As of 2022, Ryan is the CEO of seven different businesses doing 7-8 figures a year in revenue. In his real estate career he's flipped 500+ homes and currently owns 550+ rental units. As a content creator he has amassed 1.5M+ followers and has generated over 500M views.

Ryan lives in Las Vegas, NV with his wife Mindy and two children James and Olivia. Before his business success he was a professional baseball player with the Oaklands A's. His desire is to share his story, inspire others, and teach anyone how to create wealth and freedom.

Printed in Great Britain
by Amazon

37904484R00126